Will Harris of St. Paul
1932

DEADLINES

BY

Henry Justin Smith

BEING
THE QUAINT, THE AMUSING,
THE TRAGIC MEMOIRS
OF A NEWS-ROOM

HARCOURT, BRACE AND COMPANY

NEW YORK

Copyright 1922
HENRY JUSTIN SMITH
Chicago

Contents

	Page
The Day	1
In The Cave of Tongues	25
The Star	41
The Drunkard	55
Young-Man-Going-Somewhere	69
The Cub	85
The Old Man	97
The Poet	113
The Ghost	125
The Socialized Copy-Boy	143
The Triumphant Comma-Hound	161
Josslyn,—(Part One)	179
Josslyn,—(Part Two)	207
The Late Watch	231

{I}
The Day

[1]

T is still dark in the streets, still dark among the flat roofs of our block, when the day begins.

It is a winter morning before seven o'clock. Night clings to the city. Windows in some of the tall buildings burn with a radiance never extinguished; others spring into color ahead of the belated sun. On street cars and elevated trains that sail through the darkness like lighted ships the seven o'clock workers are arriving "downtown." They are shabbier, more morose, than those who come later. It is hard to be buoyant before seven o'clock in the morning.

In the newspaper office desks and long tables stand in a twilight due to glimmerings that penetrate through the windows. Typewriters, grotesquely hooded, lie in ranks. Waste-baskets yawn. The wires, clinging to the desks, are asleep; telephones have not yet found their tongues. The electric contact with the waking world is in suspension. What happened yesterday? What will happen today? The wires do not care.

A sleepy boy, shivering, his shoes trickling melted snow, enters the spectral room, carrying a bundle of morning newspapers which he lets fall upon a table. He sighs. He turns an electric switch, and the desks and tables spring into outline. The boy stares about him, stumbles over a waste-basket, kicks it away, sits in a battered chair in front of the mouth of a tarnished copper tube that runs through the ceiling, and drowses. He has barely settled down when he hears men coming in, and starts up. The men are two; young, but with graying hair. They have not much to say to each other. They do not even glance toward the boy. With a manner somewhat repressed, but alert enough, they go to desks, call out for the morning papers, and start slicing them up with scissors. Ten minutes go by, while the clock ticks serenely and the windows become grey with creeping daylight; daylight that sifts down among the roofs and through veils of smoke and fog, that comes cold and ashamed and reluctant. It envelops in new shadows the bowed shoulders of the two young men, touching their cheeks with its own pallor, casting pale reminders upon the papers they are cutting. One man glances over his shoulder at the clock. The clock presently strikes a puny but peremptory "Ping!" It is seven o'clock. The day has begun.

Now enter through the swinging door, which flies back and forth impatiently, the staff. For some time the tramping of their feet, the sound of their breathing, their low laughter, the swish and creak of the door, fills the room. There are ruddy, careless fellows in this company, sanguine youths to whom strain and difficulty are nothing. They tramp, tramp, past the desks and tables, doff overcoats, strip the typewriters of their hoods, whistle, wink at each other, take final puffs of forbidden cigarettes, chuckle together over amusing things in the morning papers, and meantime remain secretly alert—for what? Not merely for the calling of a name by the city editor (now established at his desk and scowling at clippings). Not merely for the chatter of a telephone bell, which may mean a day's work for some or all. The possibilities are vague. The tingling of blood means only that this is a new day. Something is bound to happen. They do not mention this to each other. It is against the code for one man to say to his mate: "John, this may be a momentous day. It may bring fame to someone. This may be our great opportunity." Instead, one reporter stretches and yawns: "Well, here we are again, boys; back in the old squirrel cage, to do a few more turns for the antique Press. What of it? Say, do you suppose such a thing could happen as that I'd get an interesting assignment? Where's the bird who said newspaper work was exciting? . . . ."

They are like hunting dogs, pretending to be asleep, but with their ears cocked for the mysterious, the shapeless approaching event that is in the spirit of the day.

[II]

THE room is now full. In this loft, some ninety feet long by thirty wide, place is found for nearly forty men. At one end, the end farthest from the thunder of "L" trains, sits the city editor, surrounded by assistants, tables, telephones, filing cases, wire baskets, spindles, and boys—in that order of usefulness. Within elbow distance are the copy-readers, whom the city editor both prizes and reviles. They bend over their long, battered desk, some of them chewing tobacco unobtrusively, and jab with their pencils at piles of manuscript, giving it an earnest and sardonic scrutiny. Just beyond them sit the telegraph editors, older men and more solemn of face, as befits those whose judgment grapples with majestic cables and Washington dispatches. The chief of these worthies presides at a roll-top desk upon which boys periodically dump a mess of Associated Press sheets, damp from their passage through the tube. The desk has pigeon-holes crammed with dusty reports, statistics, speeches not yet delivered, and biographies of men not yet dead. The telegraph editor is just now arguing with the head proofreader over the spelling of a Russian name. The argument waxes hot. We pass on.

There is a group of desks pertaining to the three men who attend to the "make-up"; two of the arm-chairs vacant because their owners are in the composing room. And there is a large and excessively dusty desk before which, with his back to its intricate recesses, sits the news editor, from whom are supposed to issue ideas, solutions, and enthusiasm. None of them have issued from him thus far; but the day is still young.

Behind all this is the ampler space occupied by the staff. Three reporters, sprawled over their typewriters and strings of clippings, are doggedly pounding out "re-writes" of morning paper articles. Two more are deciphering notes of matters they have just heard over the telephone. Four others stand by a window, engaged in brisk discussion. Are they discussing politics, prurient plays, or prohibition? None of these things. One overhears: "I doubt if Wells is such a scream in England as he is in America. Now, when it comes to Compton Mackenzie——"

A boy approaches one of these reporters and says, triumphantly:

"Wallace, Mr. Brown wants you."

"Right."

The literary causerie continues during Wallace's absence. He returns, pulling on his gloves. A stir among the unassigned.

"I've got to interview Sir Scammon Scammonton. LaSalle station."

"Sorry for you. Must be dull day."

"It is," grimaces Wallace, swaggering off.

A dark-haired reporter sits penciling lines upon rough paper, and looking out dreamily into the hurly-burly of traffic and over the chaos of cornices and water tanks visible from the window. He is far, far away from all this. The lines he scrawls are mystical, tender. He is a poet. And he is a very good reporter but his habits——

A stout man in a corner is writing: "It is understood that the non-partisan element in the county board——" but half his thoughts are upon Japanese prints. He is an amateur of Japanese prints.

In another corner a tall and slightly grey-haired reporter stabs with his cane at a vagrant cockroach, while shadows of reverie and discontent flit across his face. He was lately in Europe, whence he returned in disgust, shouting for the "good old life." Now he is yearning for Europe again. A novel that he began to write lies, yellowing, in a corner of his desk. He would like to go to Mexico, or to California. He applies every week for some trip or other. Meantime he meticulously does what he is told to do.

And then, there is a Cub, who sits bolt upright before his idle typewriter, eagerly, lovingly watching the distant city editor from whom today—yes, this very day—may come that "good assignment." Something exciting. Good Lord, if they would only let him——

It is a dull day, yet there is a resistless movement of the commonplace which at last pulls nearly all these men from their trifling or their brooding and sends them out into the city, out into the slushy and gloom-fast streets, out into the enormous glittering skyscrapers, to run down little events. They scatter, with their various moods of hope, disgust, scorn, or vivacity, to thread their way through the city.

The office, emptied of the staff, retains only the "desk men." These are now a little relaxed. Not only has the day's program been laid down, as far as possible, but the first edition, which has furnished a few minutes of tension, is on the presses. From regions far below there comes a muffled thunder, a jarring that faintly shakes the desks. In the news-room silence, compared with the recent pecking of typewriters and murmur of voices, prevails. The desk men straighten up in their chairs, sigh, and stretch. One of them pulls from a drawer a thick novel and reads.

It is a pause. But during this pause life goes on, climaxes prepare. Something draws nearer.

The managing editor, a heavily-built being with

harsh spectacles, prowls into the room, gazes about and halts, watched apprehensively by a benchful of small boys. He disregards the juvenile array and swings heavily, thoughtfully, over toward the desk of the news editor.

"What's doing?" he demands, in that voice whose cadences can convey so much wrath, so much bitterness—and so much sweetness.

"Nothing 'special."

"Humph!" exclaims the Old Man, and retires to his den.

[III]

THE Old Man has officially stigmatized the day as dull.

Boredom is the word.

Take a score of keenly sensitized men, confront them with routine, and the result is boredom. However, they can endure this, just as they are able to stand severe and long-continued excitement. To those who most tremble with suspense or burn with pride there comes the profoundest lethargy; but they have learned to swim in it without impairment of the spirit. Here is a faculty which they have in common with musicians, actors, and other artists. These men in the news room have traces of the creative temperament, which hibernates, then springs up with new vigor. In some of them it is faded, grown old, or hidden behind stoicism. But in the oldest and most morose of the "desk men" there lives a spark of dramatic instinct, which lights the weariest face at the coming of a "good story."

Nothing of the kind now animates them. They labor on in an incessancy of tasks which must be done at once, even though scarcely worth doing. They must be rapid and skillful without being driven by interest. Throughout the newspaper plant a finely-timed engine, deftly blended of the human and mechanical, is turning, turning. Everything must move: The grotesque arms of the linotypes, the lumpishly-moving tables of the stereotypers, the gigantic, glistening coils of the presses, the rolling sidewalks upon which the finished papers slide toward the delivery wagons. All must turn with the clock-tick. It makes no difference whether the day be dull or thrilling. The relentless machinery waits for its injections of human intelligence. The world waits for the news. And always, among these men in the newsroom, there is a dim sense of the mechanisms forever at work below them, a tinge of fear lest, through some fault, there be a break in the process, a dreadful pause in the endless tune. So, driven by habit and by their sub-conscious perception of their membership in the whole activity of the building, they contribute by pencil-strokes, by orders, by corrections on proofs, to the flow of this activity.

As the half-hours pass and the day mounts to its meridian, there is a tensing of effort. Almost casually, two editions have already been issued, inspected and forgotten. But now one can feel the climb toward a greater enterprise, the "home edition," the daily bugbear whose tradition is that it must be more comprehensive and correct than either of its predecessors. There is no more lassitude along the copy-desks; the piles of unread manuscript mount too fast. The staff is back, for the most part, and the spatter of typewriters deluges the silence. Boys run by with clumsy steps. Bells ring. The air hisses in the pneumatic tubes. The long, low room echoes to a thousand movements, a thousand utterances. Yet despite the *forte* of the news-room, one is aware of the *fortissimo* of the city itself. For outside of the newspaper office, as well as within it, the day is at its height. Skyscrapers now are belching out lunch-hour crowds, and the shopping streets are filled with joyous, vivid streams of people. Messages from this turbulence reach the newspaper office; cries come across the roof tops; the symphony of the city, with its roars, whistles, bellowings, arrives modified but clear. And if one puts his ear to the wires he can fancy that he hears the shrill and terrible voices of a hundred other cities where life seethes, even though "nothing is happening." One has a vision of potentialities of achievement or of disaster in these agitated centers of life. Straight out of the seeming commonplace of their movement in pursuit of tasks or fun will emerge the dramatic shock that the news-room is waiting for. Something is bound to happen.

[IV]

SOMETHING does happen.

First there is the sharp outcry of the Associated Press telephone, distinct from all the other bell-signals. The telegraph editor picks up the receiver and listens. Without a quiver of lips or eyebrows he reaches for paper, and scrawls. The vigilant news editor sees the rigidity of his shoulders, the slight gleam of his eye, and rises. The copy-readers look up. An instinct awakened by tiny signs, too tiny for the eye of laity, warns "the desk" that this bulletin has a high voltage.

The news editor stands reading as the hand of the telegraph editor traces:

"Washtn . . . bomb on steps . . . treasury building . . . 2 killed."

The telegraph editor hangs up the receiver. For an instant he and his chief stare into each other's eyes. But nothing is said. The implications of this message are self-evident.

"Ask Mr. Barlow to come here," the news editor murmurs to a boy.

While the boy skates nonchalantly off, the editor, with a hand that cannot keep pace with his brain, is writing notes that fly from his pad to distant parts of the building. Simultaneously he is calling earnestly on the house telephone for the circulation department.

Barlow, the make-up editor, enters, heavy-set, frowning at being called from his nearly-complete pages of the home edition. At his heels treads easily but ominously the Old Man, whose presence pervades the room like fate.

The news editor flies at Barlow and mutters to him a paraphrase of the bulletin, which by this time is being masticated by a linotype machine. Barlow's frown vanishes. He gives an eager nod, seizes a just-written sheet of paper headed "eight-column line, rush extra," and takes it with him as he makes long, heavy strides toward the composing-room door. His mind's eye has mapped out a new first page. At the door he stumbles against a boy and leaves behind him an echo of brief profanity.

The Old Man is told the news.

"I thought it would happen some day," he remarks. He eyes calmly the "telegraph desk" where now two men are working frantically, while another takes more bulletins from the telephone. Elsewhere in the room there is little commotion. The usual group of reporters are arguing the usual topics. "Peck-peck" goes the Cub's typewriter, grinding out some trifle or other.

Suddenly the young city editor emerges from his nest of telephones and comes down the room at a half-trot.

"They've tried to blow up the federal building here," he snaps, with a half-joyous, half-bitter gleam in his eyes. He dashes back to his desk, followed by the shadowy bulk of the Old Man.

The news editor begins to swear, and laughs instead, having in mind Barlow and his forms. "This will finish him," he thinks, as he speeds toward the composing room. Out there he finds Barlow and his assistant under full steam "breaking up the paper," ordering gleaming stacks of type about, shouting at printers above the perpetual clackety-swish of the linotypes, crossing out and writing in words upon the "schedules" that name the leading articles for various pages. The coatless printers paw the type with their blackened fingers, chew tobacco, and register unconcern. Type lies strewn, in bundles of lines, all over the "stone." Long galleys of brass are piled up like cord-wood. Up to the high, glass-roofed ceiling resounds the turmoil of the "stone." The battered clock points imperturbably to 12:05. And at 12:25 all this puzzle must be cleared.

Taking Barlow by the elbow, the news editor speaks in his ear. The color surges into Barlow's face. Still speechless, he darts to the half-complete first-page "form," and roars at the printer whose hands are flying over its columns. The printer hears and nods. He must change everything. What of it? All in the day's work. But the composing-room foreman, sauntering up, tosses in the remark, "Tearin' up again? You'll never make it," and with a wave toward the clock, passes on.

"We've got to make it, Jim," the news editor cries after him. Then, like a man watching two boiling kettles at once, he hastens back to the news-room.

Within the last two minutes the news-room has been transformed in spirit. Everybody has straightened; everybody has caught the stroke. Who said newspaper work was monotonous? seems to shine from the faces. It is gorgeous. The telegraph editor and the city editor are in two separate whirlpools of movement. Boys rush at the telegraph editor and slam sheets of copy upon his desk; the man at the telephone shoves scribbled slips toward him. He rapidly assembles and groups these, discarding some, piecing others together, laboring with his whole mind to form a story sequential and lucid. A series of flashes are passing through his mind: "Doubt if they'll get this bulletin in. . . . There'll be an awful mess for the next edition." And farther back in his mind occur thoughts more private, such as: "That rumor the other day about the reds was right," and "I suppose the wrong man will be caught, as usual." But his routine brain-cells, his hands, go on shaping, shaping. And save for an out-thrust lower lip he betrays no agitation.

The city editor is twice as busy as this. He has had to scratch off a dozen lines of copy for the home edition, to dispatch six men to the federal building, answer (and get rid of) three persons wanting to know if he was "posted," listen to general orders from the Old Man, alter a headline that did not "fit," and map out a sort of program for the rest of the day. His mind is ablaze with enterprise and pierced with apprehensions. Who knows but a rival paper has already beaten him? He *will not* be beaten. He sends out to every part of himself a desperate signal to function, to be alive. His tongue is dry; his voice threatens to scream. He is at bay, fighting an invincible alliance of enemies: The clock, his rivals, the tangle of things to do, his own rebellious nerves, the nerve reactions of everybody else. He calls upon his uttermost reserve. He is four men in one. He is enraged at life—but he is deliriously happy. And there flits through him a wan joke: "I suppose the police will call it a sewer-gas explosion." The joke, which goes unspoken, is extinguished by a wave of perception, vaguer than these words, but suggesting to him that society is a brutal and turbulent thing, and bringing to him like a passing flash of the cinema, a picture of the federal building portico in ruins, and of bodies lying there.

Through all this pierces the realization that the home edition has gone to press. The turmoil around him is no less, but here is the face of his friend, the news editor, emerging from the delirium.

"How's it going, George?"

"All right," he hears himself reply.

Wallace, the reporter, leans up against the desk.

"Well, boss," inquires Wallace with a subdued twinkle, "how much on the great Sir Scammon Scammonton? He says——"

The city editor becomes aware of Wallace, and halts him with:

"John, jump down to federal building . . . take taxi . . . forget about that damned lord——"

Wallace is off, murmuring quaintly: "I obey, boss, I obey."

City editor to news editor: "They think there are six dead down there. A delivery wagon was blown up. There are pieces of horse all over the street. The district attorney says——"

"We'll have to make four separate stories of it for the First Final. At least four——"

"I know. It's a big plot, of course. Oh, is that Billy on the wire? Give him here."

The news editor moves on, devoting a glance to the bowed backs of the local copy-readers, to whom the fury that began with the telegraph desk has now been transmitted. Their eyes bulge with the interest, the horror, of what they are reading. One counts with his fingers the number of letters required for a certain heading. A book that another, a placid, grey-haired man, was reading, has fallen to the floor, and lies open at the title page, "Growth of the Soil."

Reporters who have come in already from the explosion are mauling their typewriters, slamming the cylinders back and forth with a rattle like rifle fire. A constant yell of "Boy!" Dust, colored by the pale noonday sunlight, swims, serene and beautiful above their heads. Murmurs, chucklings, imprecations mingle in a flow of sound; the expressions of the fever that has seized the staff. They are painting, painting. The picture will be hurled out into the streets, seen, and lost. All are artists now, co-operating on the big canvas of the First Final. They are instinctively making art of it, discarding, heightening and coloring. Yes, they color some things, so that the hasty reader can tell them as more important than others. Maybe they do not distort facts; they do not so much distort as rearrange. They suggest perspectives, and introduce good lighting for this tale of tales.

All the while, into their hands is being poured more material, and more. The wires say that the nation is aroused. "The White House has let it be known that . . ." The wires sing with theories, conjectures, revelations. The tragedy here at the federal building is in the foreground. A notebook has been found among the rags of one of the corpses, with code words in it. Wallace is reading sentences from this book over the 'phone. The district attorney is giving out a long statement. Every minute a member of the staff enters with details which he regards as "bigger stuff than anything." Evidently the mystery of this story is deeper than we thought. It will be unraveling itself for days. We shall be pestered with it for days. What a plague! But what joy!

Meantime, behold it is two o'clock, and the First Final stares us in the face. Ah, here comes the Old Man. "The composing room is swamped." We thought so. "Throw away everything except explosion stuff." The market reports must go in uncorrected. The speech of a distinguished guest at a luncheon goes on the floor. The Cub has written five hundred words about scenes at hospitals and is told he is a fool.

The inexorable clock — the damnable, gliding clock. The waiting machines. The waiting world.

We are desperate men.

We go to the "stone" to make up the First Final. Once more, chaos; bigger heaps of galleys, greater muddles of type. Parts of stories are lost; parts of others are still lagging on the linotypes. We lose our heads, and quarrel. We become children, and say: "Who's blaming me for it?" "I told him to do it." "Good God, this gang is going to pieces."

The type pours to the "stone" from all sides. The pages lie, broken, hopeless.

This time we shall never "get out."

And suddenly we find that it is all done. The forms are full. The last one is being locked up, and slid into the outstretched hands of the stereotypers.

We glance at each other, wipe off sweat, and grin.

[V]

THIS is a splendid product of ours, after all. The boys are bringing in papers, staggering under the bundles. We spread them out on the desks, admire and criticize. It is scarcely possible we did this. Thirty minutes, twenty minutes, ago we were writing the words that now peer at us from the pages, faintly familiar creations that have arrayed themselves in a manner distinctively their own. It is all there as we planned it in our frenzy. The house has risen from that chaos at the "stone." The event that has shaken the country's nerves lies there embodied in types of varying blackness and size, making a structure with girders and gables, with foundations and flourishes. A structure nevertheless built to last but a day, to outlast scarcely even our pride in it.

Our pride in it is momentary. We are conscious that we have conquered. This feeling is confirmed when our rivals are brought in, and their paltry efforts to keep pace with us are seen. But we are too wise, or too weary, to gloat more than for that moment. Tomorrow may snatch this triumph away from us. And besides——

It is the Old Man's voice:

"Look here, we say in this head that three wheels of the wagon were blown off; but in the eye-witness account it says——"

And he lays a broad thumb upon the column.

Two or three men, among them the city editor, respectfully examine the discrepancy.

"There's always something to spoil it all," grumbles the Old Man, and bears his newspaper away, grasped in both hands, while the staff exchanges rueful winks. The city editor slips on his coat and says savagely to the news editor: "If I don't show up tomorrow you can guess why." His eyes burn in his pale young face. He flings himself out, biting off the end of a cigar. The eyes of the grey-haired copy-reader follow him humorously, tenderly.

The news editor turns to the disposal of matters for the afternoon. The greater part of the afternoon still remains. There are still "late developments." There will be a "rush hour extra." The news editor walks back through the room, remarking to the "desk" as he goes: "Nobody off early today. We'll need all hands."

They look up, unamazed. Were it to go on forever, they would still be unamazed.

[VI]

BUT at last it is five o'clock, and the very last extra of all has been patched up, and there is nothing more to do.

Darkness has come again. It seems now to have been scarcely ten minutes since the first of those alert figures entered through the swinging door; but the evidences of a complete day are all about: Waste-paper ankle deep around the desks; waste-baskets crammed with torn newspaper sheets; pencil-butts, proofs, crumpled notes.

The men, the last of them, are putting on hats and coats and departing. They go wearily and sulkily. The emotional storm in which they have been tossed has left them chilled. The more thrilling the day, the more leaden its close. This product, conceived with such skill and speed and evolved with such a fury of zeal, is already scarcely more than waste-paper. The men tramp gloomily into the hall, turning up the collars of their overcoats and peering into the shadows of the gloomy corridor. They go down the elevator, grumbling, but still with a vestige of elation.

"Well, that was *some* day," they mutter.

"*Some* day," echo the dying voices of the linotypes.

"*Some* day," groan the presses from the basement.

The men, slackened in spirit, cynical about it all, exuding revolt, are happy in spite of everything. "*Some* day," to be sure. They will tell their wives and children about it. They will meet acquaintances who will respectfully ask their opinions, because they are newspaper men.

There are new furrows in their faces; but their youth is inextinguishable.

The grey-haired copy-reader, who is last to leave, watches them go, turns out a light or two, and slowly prepares for the street. And he thinks about these men, whom, in a way, he loves:

"I wonder what draws them into this game? I wonder why they keep at it, the game being what it is. I wonder what the fascination of news is. I wonder what news really is. . . .

"The continuousness of it all; the knowledge that no matter what we do today, we must do better tomorrow. . . .

"The unendurable boredom; the unendurable excitement. . . . .

"Maybe we stay on because life is like that, and we get more of life here than somewhere else."

[VII]

THE only lights remaining are two that burn dispiritedly at either end of the long room. The wires sleep again, oblivious of the sparkling, but dreadful world. The battlefield is deserted.

Now enter two sad-faced, elderly males in soiled and shapeless clothing, carrying large sacks. Into these they dump contents of waste-baskets, and bundles of scraps. They seem very, very old and depressed. In and out among the desks they go, muttering to themselves, and clearing away the dull traces of the splendid task. These specters know nothing of the efforts or the victories just recorded. The voices of the city, the cries of newsboys, the tootings and tinklings of the streets, are nothing at all to these aged scavengers. Outlived .... all outlived.

Having finished their funereal task, they go out and the room is left to its memories, the wires to their slumber.

So ends the day.

[II]
In the Cave of Tongues

[I]

FOUR stories removed from the news-room, but connected with it impalpably in a thousand ways, is our haunt.

This haunt is a cigar store which faces the street from our building, and is indeed often mistaken for our front door. In winter storms we turn up our collars and skate joyously the ten paces distance, plunging into the warm fog of the store like sheep in a blizzard. In summer we go hatless and stand languidly in the door of the place, or sit on the benches within, sheltered from the sun. At all times we talk. There is no place like this for talking with unbridled tongues.

The cigar store has no plate-glass cases, no leather-covered chairs, no polished metal, no pretty pictures. It is ancient, foul, dilapidated, frowsy. Around its walls run the benches, which are covered with moth-eaten carpet. Benches and floor are strewn with burnt matches, bits of paper, and dried mud. In the misty windows hang limply on wires a few story-magazines, while in other conspicuous spots stand theater posters, signs advertising many species of cigarettes, and piles of "peppy" reading. In ridiculous contrast, the ceiling is lofty and handsomely carved. Once, in a prior incarnation, this was a bar-room. Now it is a store, with the pressroom just beyond a partition.

A single case contains the cigars. It is heaped promiscuously with boxes of cheap smokes, chewing-gum, and candy. In a clear space the vivacious proprietor shakes endless dice with noisy patrons.

We sit on the benches in this cave, and are utterly at home.

[II]

NOON of a winter day has passed. The home edition has just been "sent away." The lunch hour has released not only men from the newsroom, but an assorted lot from other departments. Here are several printers, one in mammoth overalls, another in cheviot but without collar or tie, still another properly clad, except his feet, upon which he wears the shattered, comfortable shoes that ease his work. Present also are two or three wagon drivers, sharp-faced youths whose cheeks bulge with tobacco, whose overcoats are drawn in by belts, and whose legs are shapeless with padding. Elbow to elbow with these are several sleek young advertising men, with their cigarettes.

We of the news-room sit a little apart, as befits our caste. With unseeing eyes we gaze at the group shaking dice. The spasmodic "click" registers nothing to us, accustomed as we are to the whole bedlam of noises within and without the store. For we are habituated to this haunt, and to this street, just as the forester is habituated to his forest and hears nothing, unless by an effort, of the poem of sighing trees, crooning insects, and twittering birds. There is nothing noticeable by us in the street, where the elevated trains flee by with insane clatter, where trucks and street cars manage a slow progress under the spur of profane warnings, and where the tread of people is heavy and constant. Even a fire-engine can pass, with its inspired shriek, and scarcely we lift an eyelid.

The city is our cradle, and its song is a soporific. We sit pondering this thing or that, oblivious to the chatter about us, lazily annoyed at the clamor of the dice-shakers. There is really only one important thing, besides keeping our cigars and pipes aglow. It is that the badly-hung door of the wretched cave persists in hanging ajar after each person comes in, and the draft chills our ankles.

"Shut the door!" we yell.

Somebody goes out. Of course, he has left the door ajar.

"There, that damn fool has left it open again."

It is our sole grievance. Someone must sulkily rise and push the door to, and then upon the next arrival the process must be repeated. It intensifies our disbelief in the progress of the human race. More and more sulkily we smoke, and smoke, and smoke.

[III]

THERE are three of us sitting in a row—Brown, the city editor, Barlow, the make-up editor, and myself. All three are still a trifle dazed, a little breathless, from the effort of "sending away the home edition." It was no worse than usual, but it was worse than the devil. The memory of those exasperations is fading now, but they have left us feeling battered and uneasy.

Barlow, his full body held erect and his cigar sticking straight out, has shrouded himself in reticence. The city editor crosses and uncrosses his legs, and murmurs:

"I got a bit excited up there. It's the very hell to get excited like that. Always say things I regret."

This is an oblique apology to Barlow, who emits a muffled sound, ambiguous but probably amiable. We judge, rightly, that the incident beginning at "the stone" is closed. There are twenty such incidents a day.

"My wife says," goes on the city editor, "that I'm too well-balanced. 'You're so well-balanced,' she complains, as though it was a crime. She gets mad because I don't fly out and break things at home. Imagine that!"

"Shut the door!" someone bawls. There are grins among the drivers, and a subdued voice: "Them cold-blooded editors."

"It's indifference, plain indifference, that makes me seem so well-balanced," further explains the city editor. "I don't get worked up enough even here, maybe. The Old Man says, 'You're so damn calm.' Well, if I am, it's because I don't attach much importance to little things. Big ones, either. I don't care if the staff quits, I don't care if we get scooped, I wouldn't mind if the paper went bankrupt, or the whole population got smallpox, or the human race went and got itself hung."

(A flicker of a smile on Barlow's face.)

The city editor, continuing: "When I say I don't care, I mean that when I'm taking my rest, between nightmares, I can let myself down into a pile of soft cushions of absolute apathy about the fate of anybody or anything. It's a great rest. It bores one, but it's a relief. There's no such vacation for the mind as being totally bored."

"The trouble with us," I suggest, "is too much neurosis."

"Too much adrenal gland," corrects the city editor.

Barlow takes his cigar from his mouth and is listened to.

"Too much of everything except income," says he, and restores the cigar.

"That," says the city editor semi-officially, "is

a matter to be taken up with the Old Man." Clearing his throat, he proceeds: "But the real question is, how to face life; that's it, how to face life. Whether to take it hard or easy. Whether to let your imagination build up tremendous obstacles, and then go around breathing like an exhaust pipe fancying you're overcoming them, or just to take things as they come and go smilin' through. I was taught to do the latter, but"—he strikes another match—"somehow it doesn't work."

"And no wonder," growls Barlow.

"No, it's no wonder," assents the news editor. "Say, boys, when you figure what our life is like, how we're forever straining ahead, looking out for the least little atom of possibility of a blunder and realizing that we've only one chance in a thousand of getting through a day without a kick, why . ."

"Incidentally, are we all hooked up to cover that hanging tomorrow?" I inquire.

"Absolutely. As I was saying, we being aware that we are born to trouble, and our luck is usually no good, what's the chance of our being optimists? Poor. Now . . ."

"Here comes a chap who's a regular walking Pollyanna," mutters Barlow.

"Oh, that's only an advertising solicitor. He's got to look that way."

The newcomer enters, eyed by the participants in an interrupted dice game, selects a cigar, lights it, flips the skirts of his overcoat airily out into the street and vanishes, pursued by shouts of "Shut the door!"

We have lost the thread of our conversation. The crowd and the smoke seem thicker, as we muse. An elderly printer is heard to say, "The dentist claims I'll feel better when they're all out." We smoke.

[IV]

A GUST of wind, a momentary louder roar from the street, and a long-legged youth, hatless, bursts into the store, laughing.

It is the Cub. He seats himself circumspectly at a little distance from us, cocks his cigarette at the same angle as Barlow's cigar, and inspects his finger-nails. We do not notice him; yet his entrance has somehow affected the turn of our thought. For the worse, too.

"Here we are, in this poisonous old cave, worn out, tired of it all, glad to be let breathe," grumbles the city editor. "Another edition to think about in half an hour. Why aren't we over at some club, lolling over our coffee and cigars, and maybe organizing a billiard game? Why aren't we streaking for the 2:15 train with our golf clubs?"

"Why don't we go into advertising?" demands Barlow.

"Or insurance——"

"Or selling bonds."

"Anything—anything that would make a fellow feel like a white man. This news game is like being caught in a fly-wheel by the sleeve. It whirls you around like a plaything, cracks you bit by bit, and throws you aside, limp and shattered. Why . . ."

I observe the bright, scandalized stare of the Cub, and interpose: "A great game, all the same."

Barlow and the city editor simultaneously remove cigars and expectorate.

"Where does it get you?" scoffs a listener.

"Yes, where?" from the city editor. His gloomy gaze encompasses the Cub, and he impulsively flings a question:

"You, kid, where do you expect the newspaper business to land you?"

The Cub, startled at being addressed, gulps, drops ashes, then replies, blushing.

"Why—I'd like to be London correspondent."

(Titters from the listening group of printers.)

"To London! Is that all? Think you can become Young-Man-Going-Somewhere in three months? Sinful Goode, eh?" But some memory of his own lost ambitions, perhaps, brings a kindlier note into the city editor's voice. "Kid," he says, "that's where we all wanted to go—once. Certainly. We would all be London correspondents, or something, if . . . It's all right. Dream on."

The Cub says nothing.

"Did you ever ask for a foreign job?" I challenge the city editor.

He emits a cloud of smoke and makes indirect reply:

"If they find you can do a desk job, then that's what you do!"

"How about Josslyn?" I pursue.

"Ah, Josslyn!" murmurs Barlow.

"Josslyn!" echoes the city editor, as though the name had a mysterious background. "That was an exception. Yes, that was a rare case. And look how it ended. You know the story, H. J.?"

"Yes," I own.

"I'd like to hear it," ventures the Cub, edging closer.

"No," says the city editor, emphatically. "Not now; not here." He glances at his watch, uncrosses his legs, and brushes ashes from his knees. It is apparent that not only the printers, but others, are listening to our jawing. The dice-game has languished. Shall the story of poor Josslyn be thus published to the world. Our delicacy says no.

Thus we are about to lift our seance. But suddenly there is a commotion at the door, the usual blast of cold air, a subtle animation in the air, and there appears a gallant figure in a tan camel's-hair overcoat. He carries a heavy, crook-necked cane, and his grey hat is tipped fetchingly over one eye. On the way to us he delivers a separate greeting to each of the elderly printers. He taps Barlow on the knee with his cane, winks at the

Cub, and brings up before the city editor with: "Hello, boss!"

It is the Star, come to cheer us.

It is our radiant Best Writer, who travels dazzlingly an orbit we cannot follow, who gives us hope of what we may become or cheats us with thoughts of what we might have been. Delightful fellow. Exasperating fellow!

The cigar dealer hails him with: "Shake you one flop, Larry; two or nothing." The loungers at the counter fall aside.

"Not now," replies the Star absently. We make room for him on the bench.

[V]

"WHAT'S new?" is asked.

"Finished my play. Wrote the whole last act last night." He taps his toes carelessly with the cane.

"Sent it away yet?"

"No. Got telegram from Barrymore, though. Interested as hell. Wired him back: 'Send four hundred expense to New York.' I think he'll come through. If he doesn't, I—say, boss," at a sudden thought, "I'm garnisheed again."

No agitation at this announcement. The Star goes on, to a full audience of printers and wagon-drivers: "He hasn't a chance to collect. Beastly little tailor on Market street. It's that bill I refused to pay a year ago. You remember the suit; blue thing a dead cat wouldn't wear. Gentlemen, I could not wear the suit! A church deacon wouldn't go to his own funeral in it. A convict wouldn't be turned loose in it . . . . Well, boss, what do?"

"See the Old Man," says the city editor, laconically.

"Thought maybe you'd stand me a small loan."

"No."

"No?" The Star's smile is undiminished. "Very well, gentlemen, let us talk of other matters. Of love, say, or war, or literature. Or facing life. Let us fling up our brows, and say with Kipling (he beats time with his cane):

"My head . . . . bloody, but unbowed . . . .

"Er—how does it go——?

"I am the captain of my soul . . . ."

"Henley, not Kipling," comments Barlow.

"As you will," nods the Star. "Or Childe Harold——"

"Roland, you mean."

"Roland, naturally. I quote:

"'The hills, like giants at a hunting lay,
Chin upon hand, to see the prey at bay . . . .

"Let's see, it goes on:

"'Now stab and end the fool . . . .'

"Anyway, it ends:

'I saw them and I knew them all. And yet
Dauntless the horn to my fair lips I set,
And blew: Childe Harold to the dark tower
came.'"

"Roland, you idiot."

"Of course. *N'importe.* The theory is the same."

A pause. The drivers and printers have listened quizzically, yet with tolerance for any freakish outbreak of the editors. The Star produces a pipe, hangs it in his mouth upside down, and remarks:

"That was a swell suicide story today."

Another pause. The Cub, humbly:

"Have you written your story for tomorrow, Mr. Larrabee?"

The Star turns his mocking gaze toward the youngster.

"Who spoke? It was my conscience, perhaps. My conscience, speaking through this genteel sophomore . . . . Sir, I have not written my story for tomorrow. I shall write it when I get good and ready." He means this shot for the city editor, who remains stolid. "I abhor writing. I can't conceive why any two-legged being adopts writing as an occupation. Putting words on paper. Ugh!"

The tirade continues uninterrupted.

"In the last four months I have written three hundred thousand words for this blackguardly sheet; three complete novels, but with nothing to show for it. Nothing but a pile of letters, mostly kicks. Women say to me: 'It must be so inturresting, writing for the papers.' God! I made a speech to a woman's club. I said: 'Literature is all slop. Your favorite authors are a bunch of fakers. I am an idiot. You are all idiots, or you wouldn't listen to me.' There was no applause. I said what I thought and there was no applause. *N'importe.* I continue, nevertheless, to say what I think——"

"Don't talk nonsense," scoffs the city editor. "You couldn't live without writing."

"Or applause," from Barlow.

The Star grins. His grin fades by degrees; his face becomes plaintive.

"I need money," he says. "Heaps of money. I earn hundreds, but I must have thousands. I owe . . . . really, I can't remember. Everybody is on my notes; everybody. Garnisheed again! . . . What will the Old Man say, do you think?"

"He'll say, 'This must be the last time.' "

The Star sits up straight.

"That reminds me. Murray's in town."

This is news of real importance. The city editor looks uneasy.

"Are you sure? It couldn't have been."

"Think I could be wrong?" he scowls. "I saw him over at Chillson's."

We glance at each other. There is an odd portent in the name of Murray. Dropping my voice, I ask: "Sober?"

The Star shrugs.

"He'll be back," Barlow chuckles. He mocks: " 'I'm on the wagon now, Mr. Thain, for good.' "

The city editor makes to speak, but remains silent. Everybody is silent. The rumble from the press-room is like a surging of surf. The dice-game has been resumed, "Click-click." A great truck swaggers out from the alley, piled to the roof with bundles of the home edition. We should return to the office at once. But we linger on, with our cigar-ends white with ash. Our thoughts busy themselves, now with Murray, now with Josslyn, now with ourselves.

It is a muddle, indeed, this life of ours. We are, as we have said, disappointed with our lot. Those of us who should have been writers are now "deskmen," and those who write call writing bosh. Yet is this true! Perhaps, after all, we are in the right berths; and somehow, certainly, we are all contributing to the momentum of a vast institution, faulty but tremendous. The mass-consciousness; that is what saves us. I do not dare use this word in the Star's hearing.

[VI]

BARLOW, however, is saying:
"Think how we crawl down here every day before daylight. Think of the unspeakable alarm-clock. Oh, Lord, the alarm clock."

"Think of the next edition," says the city editor. "I'll bet we're ten columns overset this minute."

"Think of my debts," sighs the Star.

"Think how we might be lunching at the club and golfing all afternoon," says the city editor, returning to his original grievance.

"And think how they leave my stuff out all the time," comes from the Cub.

But no one hears him. Into this doleful reverie of ours, into the chorus of our pessimism (which is quite unreal) and our gossip of Josslyn and Murray (our zest in which is very real) there comes a message. We can almost hear it approaching. Indeed, we prick up our ears somehow; we hold ourselves rigid, ready to spring in response to this unknown summons.

Sure enough, a boy with a huge head and a freckled grin appears at the door. He is hatless. In his hand he carelessly holds a piece of copy-paper, with some words scrawled on it.

He peers in, then fumbles at the latch.

The city editor has already arisen. He receives the note through the door; reads: "Four-eleven fire rung in from Gloria theater. Extra?"

We read over his shoulder. A sort of wine pours into our veins. Together, three abreast, we race away, leaving behind the Star tapping his toes with his cane. A cry of "Shut the door!" follows us as we flee from the mournful voices of the Cave of Tongues, flee from our doubts and our troubles, and rush joyously toward the work we were meant to do.

{III}
The Star

[I]

THIS way, if you please. Come right through this aisle between the desks. Look out for that 'phone cord. Rather dark here. Over in this corner is the place. Have a seat. Well, now you are sitting in the Star's own chair. You find the bottom pretty hard? Well, the Star doesn't mind that. He doesn't sit in his chair very much.

This is his desk. Perfectly plain, like all the others; battered old thing with a typewriter in it that's always threatening to slip its fastenings. Not a roll-top, of course; no pigeonholes; nothing but those drawers, in which (unlocked) the Star keeps his secrets. Observe this litter on top of the desk. Faugh! These papers are dusty. He never throws anything away; just shoves the litter back and lets it lie. A lot of good ideas are penciled on some of those papers, and a lot of foolish ones mixed up with the good ones. Let 'em lie.

The old-fashioned desk-light hooded in a piece of copy paper is one of his hobbies. Without that paper it would blind his eyes. The paper is always falling off. Nuisance. But when the Old Man came by one day and growled, "Need a new desk-light, don't you" he only got the reply: "What for? What's use bothering?"

On the paper is scrawled a notice:

"Light-fingered fiend in human form who took my 'Philosophy of Love,' by Remy de Gourmont: Return or take consequences."

Look at the wall alongside the desk. He writes things on the wall; memoranda, scraps of verse, ideas. And, you see, he's pasted up a few pictures. These futurist things out of the Dial are probably his favorites. As for this poster advertising a Griffith movie, I suppose he put it up as a joke on himself, a piece of irony. That newspaper half-tone—fellow smoking a pipe—is a picture of his best friend.

Of course everything's covered with soot and smeared up with pencil-marks and the light here is vile. God knows why he likes this corner so well, but it's certain that if we gave him a place by a window, or a nice private room with a shiny desk and a push-button, he'd get peevish and wouldn't write. He likes it here in the alcove. He likes this old, smeary news-room, with its cracked plastering and its quaint shadows; and he likes the noises from outdoors when the room is quiet, the hoots and shrieks and crashes; and he likes the city, so romantically woven of the crude and the elegant, the horrible and the lovely . . . .

But I mustn't get into that vein . . . . Watch out! Oh, it's only the Star's pet mouse that lives in his desk.

[II]

PERHAPS it would be as well to stop calling him the Star—a sobriquet which he loathes—and introduce him, though absent, by his name, which is Philo Austin Larrabee. He won't stand for the Philo, and the office somehow balks at the Larrabee, so the office generally calls him Larry. He signs himself, on his stories, as Austin Larrabee.

Names seldom call up a true picture of a man. I suspect that this one suggests a matinee-idol sort of fellow, with spats and hair slicked down; or a parlor poet with horn spectacles, clothed in meekness. Larry's name is no more harmonious with him than is his desk. The desk and its environment make you imagine a seedy, alpaca-coat type of genius, with pockets stuffed full of manuscripts, smoking a corn-cob, don't they? But Larry is so little like either the horn spectacles or the alpaca coat that he would surprise you. I'll shut my eyes and get him vividly in mind, and then describe him.

Let's see. It wouldn't tell you much to say that his hair is brown, his height medium, and so on.

I believe his hair is brown; at least, I have an impression of a dark overgrowth, sometimes furiously tangled, sometimes neatly clipped and brushed. He doesn't look the same way all the time. It seems as though his personal appearance is a matter of chance. There are days when his oval face is a peaceful pink, as though from massage, and then it may be sallow, haggard, and savage. His eyes don't change, however. They glint the same blue, and the brows over-arch them with the same fine, half-oriental lines, on all days. Intelligence, humor, disdain, are uttered by his eyes; and there comes into them, rarely, a furious glow. It comes only when he works. He is most natural when braced before that typewriter, with one of his long legs drawn up under him, and the other stretched straight out, with the heel of his brightly-polished shoe grinding into the floor. He makes quick dabs, between sentences, at the hair over his left ear. Actually I believe he has worn a bare spot there with his slender fingers, upon one of which he wears a worthless ring. Often he looks up, with a curious, belligerent stare, at anyone who may be passing.

Just as his face wears different aspects, his costume undergoes the most freakish of changes. He has days when he shambles in with shameful trousers and a cap fit for a safe blower; and there are others when he arrays himself in fine linen and rich blue, and flaunts his camel's-hair overcoat and twirls a cane. There is utterly no premeditation about his clothes. He would just as soon as not wear a sweater and an old raincoat to a luncheon at the Hotel Splendo-Majestic, or parade Little Hell in afternoon dress. Clearly, he spends much money on apparel, for he is constantly surprising us with hitherto unobserved suits and overcoats and hats; and indeed he naively tells us whenever he thus invests, and adds that he has done it on the principle of "part down." His plumage is as varied as that of a prima donna. It would be useless for me, in describing him to you, to say "he wears this" or "he wears that." Except in summer. Then he demurely wears white, and his only gauds are his ties, which are a fantasy in color and color combinations, revealing more than anything else the earnestness of his search for something novel. Well, of course, there are also his shirts. Very exotic, naturally. In summer he often leaves his white linen coat hanging over his chair and strolls about the office, or even through the streets, displaying stripes like unto an awning.

On the days when his face has that pink look his walk is elastic, blithe, triumphant; on the sallow and haggard days he slumps between the door and his desk with never a wink of gayety. There are also intermediate states, grave and taciturn days, when he moves slowly at a commonplace stride, without interest. Perhaps those days are the worst, when he is neither elated by the discovery of a new costume-effect nor deliciously sunken in gloom; those days when he is apparently an ordinary being, with duties, body-functions, and bills to pay, and perhaps not a Star at all.

At all times, at his very worst, an incalculable, fascinating, graceful being, a delicately-hung organism, just a bit off balance; a boy with singular traces of age. Delacroix would have painted him with a half-starved look and his deepest frown, and his finely-modeled, half-sneering nose sharp against a dark background. I paint him for you, quivering and tousle-headed, against that smudged window-pane there, pouring his genius into a typewriter. One of us. A comrade . . . . But I mustn't drop into that vein. What time is it?

[III]

YOU ask: Who is he, after all? What does he "do on the paper?"

Well, he is a reporter; nothing but a reporter. He goes out and sees things happen and hears people talk; then he comes in and writes about them. We have twenty others who do that and do it very well. So what is it that makes Larry a star? Mark this, my friend: He is not a star because he pursues desperate criminals in an airplane, or because single-handed he extorts confessions from political grafters, or on account of this or that spectacular folly of reporting such as the cinema clownishly flashes. If we have to send somebody to ride in a locomotive cab, we send one of the "ordinary" men; one of the rough-and-tumble sort whose skins aren't worth much, and who can't write a lick.

Larry is a star because he emits rays of light. I mean—I mean his nature is a lens from which the drab colors of this earth are reflected in hues that fascinate one, confound one, and are yet real. He never sees things as anyone else sees them; we gave up long ago trying to make him do so. It is simply impossible for him to interpret life from the viewpoint of the trite and self-satisfied multitude. He cannot, to save him, lead up to a conclusion that "all's right with the world," that "to the brave belong the fair," or "boost, and the world boosts with you." As for actually uttering such a sentiment, he would commit murder first. He is death on pretenders, hypocrites, and optimists. He punctures their toy balloons by mere statements of fact, shorn of comment, but barbed by the peculiar keenness of his words. His style is very direct. Larry has discarded more circumlocutions, more "literary phrases," than the average doctor of philosophy has learned. I suspect that he has spent long, smoky hours inventing escapes from the academic. I know that he has prowled the streets day and night searching, searching for the words that would express the buildings, the people, the noises, the odors. Little words; little, torch-like words. Those are what he wants, and what he uses. Therefore, what Larry writes is very easy to read; but not naive. Oh, no! That complexity of his, that odd refracting quality that I mentioned, makes a composition by Austin Larrabee something peculiar in its effect, disturbing, prismatic.

The city editor, Brown, found it so disturbing that after Larry had worked on the paper a year he went to the Old Man about it. And the Old Man said: "Either fire him, or stop sending him out on routine assignments." So the city editor told Larry to report what he liked, and write what he liked.

There have been precedents for that sort of thing, even in our office; but it hasn't always worked out as it did with Larry. A normal human being, given complete freedom, is apt to waste it, get lazy, frazzle out. Not so our friend who occupies this corner. The new order had an unforeseen effect upon him. Brown says he started back as though he had been struck, and then snapped out:

"Want to put it all onto me, eh? All right!"

This fit lasted an hour, and then he strolled back to Brown's desk, and with one of his most fascinating and affectionate smiles he said: "Say, I believe I can write some good stories for you, old boy." He was all flushed up, and he had dabbed at his forelock until it hung in strings. Without waiting for Brown's response, he dashed back to his typewriter and in a few minutes it began to clatter like a drill.

That was the beginning of an arrangement whose fruits have astonished us all, have astonished the city itself. The city never knew it was like Larry's pictures of it. The city fancied itself busy, or noisy, or prosperous, or admirable, or monotonous; it never knew it was complex, impulsive, romantic—gorgeously romantic. It thought its buildings were handsome; it did not realize they were beautiful, beautiful with a stunningly futurist design. It thought its people were "interesting," but it never delved into the million variations of type brought here by the People of Fifty Lands. The city laughed at hundreds of "freaks," it vaguely pitied thousands of unfortunates, it flung dimes to innumerable beggars, it dreamed about scores of younger lovers, it revered many a millionaire, it shrank from jails full of criminals—but it never realized any of them. Not until Larry was "turned loose."

Larry can interpret the city because he loves it. He doesn't want to write about anything else. Say Paris or New York to him, and get a sneer for your pains. He has found the city big enough for him, and feverish enough, and beautiful enough; he has not nearly exhausted it; he has only just started. And the more he plunges into its jungle and fishes in its cesspools for the rare deposits of human treasure that make up his "stories," the more unending seems his search. Let it go on. For God's sake, let it go on. I do hope Larry won't get morose, and quit. But I mustn't be led into that vein. Who's coming in?

[IV]

I'M glad it's not Larry, for I wanted to tell you what kind of a fellow he is.

Well, he's the kind of fellow who appears to have out-grown, or cast aside, practically all the known precepts for normal living, and doesn't give a copper for anybody or anything.

Larry declares that he doesn't believe in religion or even in ethics. He takes pleasure in repudiating most of the ten commandments, the Golden rule, and a large part of the Sermon on the Mount. He uses up the time of somebody nearly every day rejecting honor in the abstract, loyalty in the rough, and such things. Most heartily he scoffs at success. He does not demean himself to ridicule such things as riches or fashion, but he does talk venomously about success, and not enviously, either. It is an inflammatory subject for him that some people attain what they want, or at least think that they have attained it. Perhaps it only maddens him because they think they are content, whereas he insists that nobody is content. Himself least of all. If he were to come in here just now, and you should say that he looks happy, you would get a tongue-lashing in Larry's best style, which would include some words you hadn't heard before.

This young man strolls through the world with a queerly bitter greeting for it, yet with an engaging smile. He asserts he hates the world, hates the human race, spurns its contrivances for being peaceable and joyous, and has no hope of it.

He says he does not believe in marriage or in honesty. But he is married and lives true to his wife. And he never stole anything.

Honor? Why, he wouldn't go back on a friend for—for all that he owes. Loyalty? Well, I can only judge of that by the way he clings to us, and the way he works. He adores Brown, who gave him his big chance. He would drag himself out of a hospital on one leg if he thought Brown needed him. When he has his little illnesses he scrawls notes to Brown, in a big school-boy hand, saying, "Don't worry. I'm sending down a story by messenger." He is loyal to us, and he is loyal to Mrs. Larry. Of course you understand that he is rather run after by foolish women, literature-mad girls who want to learn his secret of writing, and others who are plain crazy. But just let Mrs. Larry come in sight, and he shakes off the insects in petticoats and waves them good-bye. For their pains they can see Larry escorting her down the street, twirling his cane and plainly an affectionate husband.

It's bosh that he hates the human race. Or perhaps he does hate the race as such. Lots of brainy men have indulged in that large and harmless habit of hating the species, of denouncing its general attributes, its frailties, its inconsistencies, and so on. Lots of men who have a terrible vigor and a divine irritability bottled up in them let drive at people in general so as to avoid hurting people in particular. For individuals, whether encountered in small groups or large, these same men have a half-pitying geniality that frequently concentrates into acts of kindness. Look at Mark Twain. Look at Bob Ingersoll. And now look at Larry. He shouts that he despises mankind, but in all his contacts with mankind he is gentle, amiable, brotherly. Ah, he absolutely rejoices in scraping elbows with people. See him in a crowd, content with his absorption in the feeling of being among people. See him enter a room; how his face lights up; how everybody's face lights up! Maybe he hates humanity, but he is himself human.

[V]

I OUGHTN'T to have got into that vein. It would be certain death if Larry were to overhear me. . . .

Who's that mooning about by the front window, watching the city put on its paste diamonds for the evening? It's Larry, isn't it? No, it's Murray. It's only our drunkard.

There is an affinity between the Star and the drunkard. Larry pretends that he is interested in poor Chick only as a pathological case: studies his retrogression, and all that. Again his pose. Once when they were police reporters together—but Josslyn tells that story better than I do. I was only going to cite it to prove that Larry has in him that deftly guarded quality of compassion that is in all us newspaper people more or less, and that either makes great men of us—or breaks us. He does more for poor Chick than any of us do, unless it is Josslyn. Still, there may be a fascination for Larry in observing the tortuous ways of our stumbling Murray. His own mind is tortuous; his processes, too, a trifle pathological. So thin is the film that divides genius from its most terrible caricature.

* *

Where's Chick going? See him grope.
I don't suppose he's going anywhere, really.
Perhaps Larry isn't, either.

{IV}
The Drunkard
[I]

URRAY'S case started before prohibition, and continued after prohibition. So far as Murray is concerned, there is no prohibition.

It started years ago, and hasn't stopped. There seems to be no end to it. Every now and then the Old Man explodes, rolls his eyes terribly, and says there must be an end. Everybody responds, "Yes, that's right; it must be the last time." But, one by one, everybody weakens, and here is Murray back on the staff.

We are ashamed of ourselves. We are stupendously bored. The whole thing is an ungodly nuisance. Worse than that, it is a blow to our morale, it is a frightful example to the "younger men," it has no excuse even in the name of humanity. Its last shred of justification as a humane thing vanished months ago. There is no reason anywhere; nothing, not the least hypocritical, disingenuous atom of a reason, why we should have Murray back on the staff. But here he is.

Sometimes months pass without Murray. He is somewhere else, doing heaven knows what. He becomes a fiction, a legendary person who once worked here, and about whom cluster amusing reminiscences. Then one day we arrive at the office, distributing ourselves to our various desks and duties, and behold! there is a familiar sleek black head half hidden behind a morning paper, a well-known pair of pointed shoes cocked upon a chair. And Murray's half-sheepish, half-defiant grin greets us.

"Hello, Chick."

"Hello, fellows."

We shake our heads as we take up our work. To think that Murray should have come back! To think that he should have the nerve to come back! The fact is both entertaining and irksome; and it goes deeper. It is a symbol of the cycle of vanishing and returning events to which our lives are attached. The endless activity of machinery, the recurrence of the same incidents both within and without the office, the performance of the same work in the same way—it is with things like these that the resuscitation of Murray blends vaguely but pertinently. This makes the fact of his return not only entertaining, not only irksome, but curiously comforting.

[II]

OF course there must be one bad boy in every large family, one villain in every cast. And in a modernized office, where personality is better poised than it used to be, there has to be at least one "throw-back."

For the most part we in the news-room are regenerate. We are men of family, sober men. Here and there is the face of a reformed drunkard —a face sad and reminiscent. It would be unspeakably shocking should one of these older men, whose career in liquor lies so far behind as to lose even the value of anecdote, come in some morning and break the furniture. Why, he simply could not do it! The completeness with which regeneration has captured the majority of us makes the utter unregenerateness of Murray, his debonair and unashamed irresponsibility, a very piquant thing in our lives. He is like a wine goblet (time of Charles II) among a collection of Mayflower crockery. He is a story of old times. He reminds the older men of their youth.

Whenever Murray comes back, Josslyn, the grey-haired copy-reader, tells once more about the staff as it was when he was first city editor. Even the Old Man is known to unbend, and to relate how when he was a reporter. . . . Yes, sir, newspaper men were devils in those days. Why, when there was to be a hanging every man Jack assigned to "cover" it used to get drunk, and when it was over they used to come into the office roaring "Danny Deever." And say! Do you remember the First Ward Ball, that terrific annual orgy when politicians, crooks, and libertines used to keep it up until daylight, and reporters had free tickets. The day after the First Ward Ball hardly anybody could come to work. (Chuckles.)

Josslyn digs out of his archives some crude verses, written on such a day:

> The morning after the First Ward Ball
> Nary a reporter reported at all.
> And such as did wore a doleful smile,
> Nor did Josslyn's glance his dander rile.
>
> First Fox came in with half-shut eyes,
> Vowing at six he began to rise.
> He "just couldn't help the train blockade,"
> And for the Desk's mercy he earnestly prayed.
>
> Then came Jones a half hour later,
> Resembling, we thought, a half-drowned satyr.
> "I was out at the ball pretty late," he said,
> Pressing his hands to the side of his head.
>
> But poor old George never came at all—
> They found him asleep when they cleaned the hall.
> From under a table he crawled to the 'phone
> And reported for work with a piteous moan.

The First Ward Ball is no more. That generation is no more. "Hinky Dink" Kenna's place is a soft drink parlor. The stories of those days have a flavor like the anecdotes of the California gold stampede. There remains only Murray, who is not at all a physical relic of our drunkard age, but a sort of reincarnation, mysteriously alive among us, of which we have lost the secret.

In our more solemn moments we realize that he is a terrible figure. This reincarnation is something that should never have been. We ask each other earnestly, "Where does he get it?" and when we ask that we are asking a whole modern society why, if it really was determined to turn a new leaf, it did not turn it so effectively that even Murray could be "readjusted." And sometimes — usually just after he has disappeared again and "left us flat"—we bang our fists down and exclaim: "What's the use of prohibition if it doesn't prohibit?" But not often do we grow so much impassioned about anything. We have to accept Murray with all his implications; we have to reconcile ourselves, day upon day, to the fact that nothing grievous is ever cured, that this plague or that is sure to return, that laws are fifty per cent failures, and that we spend our lives accommodating ourselves to matters that are all wrong and won't grow better. So we balance ourselves in a mood of half-humorous pessimism, shrug our shoulders at irritations and grotesqueries, make epigrams upon our woes — and welcome Murray back.

"Hello, Chick. O. K. again, eh?"

"Hello, fellows. Yes, I'm on the wagon now, for good."

He is tapping out on his typewriter an article for the next edition. There is an abnormally clean and alert look about him. A subdued look, too. He has had a hair-cut, a shave, and a massage. The flesh of his face is fine-drawn, pale, refined by the suffering that has attended his latest spree, and especially by the awakening from it. His trimly-built figure wears a new, dark-brown suit that speaks of his latest Herculean effort to convince the world that this is a new Murray. He writes intensely, careful of the diction. Yes, it is all past. Nothing has happened. His body and soul went wandering in a strange spectral land with purple trees and a red sky, from which flashed eerie lightnings, and now they have come back, the same body and soul, and dropped without a jolt into the grey world of the normal, and Murray has taken up silently the routine of talking and writing. He even writes poetry. He is a wonder!

[III]

THEY say that it is now seven times that he has fallen, and has "reformed."

There is never any warning. He goes on looking just like that, a compact, nicely-dressed fellow writing clean English. He is sent out on an errand of some importance, perhaps. Then— silence. Blankness. No Murray. A typewriter that remains hooded. Letters for Murray in the mail box. "Where's Murray?" "Damn it, where's Murray today?" The city editor slams inoffensive papers and spindles around his desk. Then he smiles a smile that the men have seen before. Then he gets up and goes into the Old Man's room.

The copy-readers begin to whisper and shrug. Same old scandal. They watch Brown curiously when he comes out of the Old Man's room. Brown squares his elbows to his work. The copy-readers can reconstruct his conversation with the Old Man, even without a clew to it.

"Murray's gone again, Mr. Thain."

"Well, I told you not to take him back. Good God, how long am I going to . . ."

"But you remember I consulted you, and you said we should give him one more chance."

"Don't remember such a conversation. I've always said he was impossible. I've warned you repeatedly not to give him any important assignment. This is just plain stupidity of yours, Brown."

(A hard-breathing silence on Brown's part.)

"Where do you suppose he got it?" muses the Old Man.

"Why, you know he can get it anywhere. He's so popular they throw it at him."

(Silence on the Old Man's part.)

"Well . . ."

"Well . . ."

The days go by, and nothing is heard from Murray. It seems impossible that anybody could drop so completely from sight. Inquiry is made at his home. His wife has gone back to her parents for the third time. Nobody at the flat except a hovering swarm of bill-collectors. Mrs. Murray, when seen, says that this is the end. Her mother reinforces the verdict.

Reporters who occasionally visit bootlegging haunts tell us there is no sign of Murray. Actually it seems as though something must have happened to him this time. We are a little disturbed with each report of an unidentified body in the lake. But this fear is laughed down, and pure blankness again characterizes the case of Murray, except for those piquant anecdotes of "the previous incident." The story he went out to get has long since been obtained by some other reporter, printed, and forgotten. The mystery lasts until his reappearance, which is also a mystery.

Once or twice it has varied a little. On one occasion Murray emerged unaccountably during his headlong dive into liquor, called up the Old Man at his house at eleven o'clock at night, and asked for a loan of ten dollars. The Old Man roared at him, "I'll loan you a tub of ice, you booze-fighter!" and then started shouting "Where are you? Where are you?" But in the meantime Murray had hung up. He was gone for six weeks.

One other day of lapse he came into the office

late in the afternoon after all the editions had gone and someone else had "done" his neglected story, and insisted on writing the story himself. Brown had gone home, and Josslyn had to deal with the case. He refused to let Murray use a typewriter, so Murray went to the office of a rival paper, and asked to be permitted to write a story for us! They threw him out of that office. He went to a second, where the man in charge treated the matter humorously, led Murray to a typewriter and even loaned him a messenger boy to bring the story to our office two paragraphs at a time. Josslyn has the pieces yet.

The morning after that exploit in came Chick and upbraided Brown for not printing his article.

"You're fired, Chick," said Brown quietly.

"I—I most heartily regret to hear it," replied Murray, balancing himself carefully. He then took off his hat to the city editor's office boy, and disappeared for a month.

During two of his disappearances, as we have now learned, he went to distant cities and worked there. First it was San Francisco, then it was Philadelphia. Each time he was a faithful, reliable employe—for a while. He wrote from San Francisco to Josslyn:

"They think a lot of me here. I've got a strong tip that I'll be made city editor in a few months. Like the town fine. I haven't had any trouble about—you know. Would you mind paying a debt or two with this money-order? Larrabee and Barlow, $5 each. Keep out your own five, of course. No, I'm never coming back."

Within two weeks he appeared, very downcast. There was the usual secret session in the Old Man's room, and the usual reinstatement.

While he was on the Philadelphia paper he was sent out here to cover a railroad "strike crisis." He was very, very sure of himself. That day he came in, shook hands all around with much dignity, and told us he was going to "sign his stuff." To Josslyn he confided the fact that he and his wife were reconciled, and that as soon as he could find a flat in Philadelphia he was going to send for her. He left breezily to attend the wage conference.

In the afternoon he appeared in our office with his hair somewhat ruffled, and the satyr-like smile that often put us on our guard. He leaned against a desk, and carefully explained that he had somehow missed the conference; asked if he couldn't use our proofs to send a story east. Also he pleaded with Barlow in whispers for quite a while, but to no avail. He left jauntily, colliding with the Old Man in the hall, and saying, "Beg pardon, old chap." We heard nothing more of him for two months. Then came a telegram from the Philadelphia paper: "Look out for one Chick Murray. He may try to get job with you. He drinks."

It was after this that we made our most Herculean effort to save him. We collected a fund and sent him to the "cure." He went most humbly. He returned "cured." His wife herself brought him in, showed him to the Old Man, and tearfully thanked that august person for all he had done. Chick cried, too, and I fancy it was a near thing that the Old Man didn't cry. Murray was given his most formal reinstatement of them all, and the office advanced him two weeks' salary to pay his debts. (I've heard that the Old Man guaranteed the apartment rent for three months.) All this was just before the Volstead act took effect. Of course, everybody felt that if Chick could last until that January first he would be safe. And he did! He worked quietly and effectively far into that January, and the boys who had bet that he wouldn't were forced to pay.

Then Brown had a brilliant idea. He would send Murray out on an assignment to discover whether prohibition was being enforced. He said to him: "Look here, you know where all the joints are. You know all the bartenders. I guess you know better than to take a drink yourself. Here's some expense money. That's all."

"Yes, sir," replied Murray.

Two days later, when he hadn't returned, someone mildly suggested to Brown that perhaps he had dangled too great a temptation before the reformed drunkard, even during a prohibition regime. Brown angrily replied: "He'll come back, and sober. He's cured, ain't he? Don't anybody preach a sermon to me. That fellow knows he can't afford to break faith with George Brown."

Three days more, and behold! Murray did come back. He sat down on Brown's desk, put his arm around the city editor's neck, and made a speech, substantially as follows:

"Brown, you've been—best friend I had. I think you're greatest newspaper man in the world, Brown. Thass what I think. When all else fails, rely on good ol' Brown; thass what I say. Brown don't ever ask a feller, 'Where's that story, or those money'; does he, Brown?"

"Where is that story?" demanded Brown, throwing off Chick's arm.

Murray pulled out some silver, laid it before his chief and said, "There." He added, "Ac-kick-counting."

Just then the Old Man passed through the local room without noticing his protege. Murray craftily gained the door and vanished.

[IV]

I TELL these things not with an eye to humorous anecdote. I tell them only to illustrate the plight we have been in. We have been kind to a fellow worker, we have dared to take pity upon one who is outcast by every standard of "honorable action," and we have been paying the penalty. Why should we be cursed by Murray, the spector of Liquor?

Well, we should not be thus cursed did we not yield to this passion for taking Murray back. And so why have we yielded? It must be that there lurks in us a reprehensible secret delight in his abandonment to habits that we dare not harbor. For we cannot claim so great a natural benevolence as to endure these annoyances and countenance these broken promises, just for love. We love Murray; yes, it is true. There is a warm, glad feeling when we find him once more at his typewriter, glancing up at us with that veiled gratitude of his. But our affection will not brook everything. It must be that our subconscious passion for liberty, a passion now strangled in the company of men steadied, reconciled, tamed, takes form in the delight in Murray, who cannot prevent himself from following his appetites. He is only an intimate manifestation of a fallible world which, perhaps, we understood better than other people do. We pity it more; we tolerate it more. We know that this world has aspirations, as we have, and fails, as we do. It has not been in us to withhold forgiveness from its Chick Murrays.

Nevertheless, this is now certain:

He cannot work here any more. The Old Man has said so—despite appeals from Brown and Josslyn—and if the Old Man is not consistent, who is? And if the Old Man cannot throttle his affection for this boy, and shut the door upon him, who can? It's all over with Murray, so far as the news-room is concerned.

[V]

LATER—he's back. He isn't going to drink any more. He has paid off his debts. He has made peace with his wife. He has a new suit on, and is writing a story, very carefully. This time we think he is saved.

"Hello, Chick. Back again, eh?"

"Hello, fellows. Yes, I'm on the wagon for good, now."

[V]

Young-Man-Going-Somewhere

[I]

YOUNG - MAN - GOING - SOMEWHERE is the comrade mentioned in the first of these sketches who sat stabbing with his cane at migratory cockroaches and wishing he were—anywhere.

Most of us are reconciled to staying in or near the news-room, doing our stuff, eating lunch in the same place, going home to the same homes, and expressing generally the humdrummery of being efficient and reliable. Young-Man-Going-Somewhere—his name is John Goode, but his sobriquet is Sinful—is unreconciled. In his own way he is both efficient and reliable, but he would rather be them some other place than where he is.

He expresses for us the everlasting restlessness of our tribe, just as the Drunkard expresses our submerged liberties; and thus, requiring somebody to travel for us, since we cannot travel ourselves, we find Sinful Goode very essential. Indeed, he and his type are useful to the profession and useful even, it might be said, to civilization. For if there were not newspaper men whose souls demanded movement and exploration, and hardship and long, long trails, if there were not men whose curiosity gives them no rest, first pages would be a great deal duller than they are.

With this much superfluous reflection, let us apply our microscope to Young-Man-Going-Somewhere.

[II]

I CONFESS that I have not given you his real name. Were I to mention it you might recognize it. At least it would be well known in a certain small town where Sinful Goode was born, and where he was once expelled from the Debating Society. Between trips, I have heard, he makes surreptitious visits to his aged parents, who still live in the town; but these do not count among his globe-trottings, and he is said to come back rather saddened.

We don't really know anything about that. We do know that Goode got on our staff somehow or other about ten years ago, and that within six months he was calling the chief of police, the state's attorney, and most of the judges, by their first names. Also he seemed to know about streets that we had never heard of, and he kept making allusions to saloonkeepers, yeggmen, and Chinese tong leaders whose very existence was news to us. He must have spent his evenings just ferreting about. He was tortured by that terrible curiosity, and gifted with that faculty of making intimates, that has taken him all over the world. I suppose he calls various Japanese samurai and Russian novelists and French deputies by their first names, too.

It was after he had been here only a year that he was given his first long trip. It was to cover a revolution in Venezuela, or maybe Nicaragua. Now don't imagine I'm going to spin a yarn that Sinful Goode led the army and settled the revolution. This is not a novel. Sinful didn't do anything but send home some cables that were printed on the fourth page, and then come home himself and growl because they weren't printed on the first. But, having proved that he could live on tortillas and tarantulas, he was the logical man to go to Mexico when a revolution broke out there. The revolution was opportune, for Goode had by now developed his restlessness in full degree, and had nearly worn the Old Man to death suggesting that he sail around the world or something.

"Goode's going to Mexico," the Old Man told the city editor.

"Glad of it. Hope he croaks," replied the c. e.,

whose nerves had also been worn a bit thin by having Sinful Goode in barracks.

The rest of us were more benevolent. We gave Goode a farewell dinner, at which and to which our doggerel experts did great execution. Next day we inspected his new riding breeches, his camera, and his horrendous revolver. And then we forgot him.

It must have been that the revolution was one of those that prove more exciting in El Paso than anywhere else, for I don't recall a single story that Goode sent to the paper. The thing that does reverberate in memory was the office gossip about Sinful's expense account, which was so remarkable that not even the Old Man could keep still about it. The chief item was one horse, which Goode bought without thinking it worth while to ask permission of the office. And under the general heading of "horse" there were entries such as "food," "stabling" and "equipment." Everything at war prices, (Mex.). Everything neatly arranged in columns, and a balance at the bottom, decidedly in Goode's favor.

The Old Man, according to report, wired our new-fledged war correspondent: "Sell horse at once." The reply, which the city editor showed to some of us in confidence, was in almost these words: "Assure you no sense in selling horse at this time. Advise wait for rising market. Meantime cannot traverse this God-forsaken country on foot. If dissatisfied with my work say so and I'll go back to police reporting."

Well, the painful episode dragged itself along, to the great advantage of the telegraph company. The Old Man really was at Goode's mercy, for if a correspondent down there among the mesquite chose to argue instead of obeying or resigning, the only way the Old Man could end the argument was by wiring Sinful a discharge; and he thought far too much of the brash youngster to do that. How it all might have ended we know not; for the logical end was lost in the outbreak of the Great war, which made Mexico, Goode, and his horse seem like first-reader stuff.

Naturally, we were all frantic with work when the calamity swept down on us; and yet, from occasional bulletins that reached us from the Old Man's room, or gossip told us in chuckles by the telegraph operators, we knew that Sinful Goode was not idle.

One little file of telegrams, shown us by Bungey, the "chief operator," revealed the situation:

"Mexico City.

"Thain, the Press: Am leaving for Vera Cruz Saturday; arrive New York Thursday; can catch Baltic arrive France before German invasion; wire three thousand dollars Vera Cruz. GOODE."

"Goode, care American consul Mexico City: You have not been ordered Europe. Come home. THAIN."

"Vera Cruz, Thain, The Press: No answer received my message am sailing for New York Monday. Need money. Can borrow but request place three thousand my credit Guaranty Trust Company. Wire Washington issue my passport for France ask war department give me correspondent credentials.
"GOODE."

"Goode, care Guaranty Trust Company, New York: You have exceeded all orders in going to New York. Come home at once. Wiring hundred dollars carfare.   THAIN."

"New York, Thain, The Press: Why quibble about exceeding orders? I am logical man cover this scrap for you where can you get better? Have already engaged passage Baltic. Paid deposit my private funds. Does the Press want to be in debt to me? Have arranged with Washington my passport. Rush three thousand.   "GOODE."

"Goode, care Steamer Baltic, New York: Can see advantages your going since already gone part way. Did you get money? Take care of yourself.   "THAIN."

We all read these messages with eagerness and with awe. Not one of us could have wrangled thus with the Old Man and escaped alive. Sinful Goode, with his insubordination and his enterprise, had made the terrible Thain surrender. How we wished we had been born that way! How we envied the correspondent, joyously afloat, freighted with money and bound for the Supreme Adventure!

And yet, would we stand in his place, destined for hardship, peril and the chance of disgrace instead of glory? Would we gamble with life as did he?

Alas, we sighed, we were not born to do it.

[III]

THE war swamped us. The war sprung upon us portentous surprises, incredible emergencies. It blinded us with its horror and its splendor; and, meantime, it so involved us in new meshes of routine that we could scarcely afford time for pleasurable gossip. Thus Sinful Goode and his Odyssey became remote interests, thrust upon us only occasionally by the task of deciphering his cables.

We gathered that he managed to get arrested by the Germans in Belgium; that he argued his way to freedom and then argued himself into favor with the advance French troops. One story told us how he watched the first bombardment of Rheims as he lay among the waving grain; another how he observed an engagement from the roof of a shell-torn house. Later—we scarcely knew whether it was months or years—he was fleeing from Antwerp among the refugees; again, he was at Dunkirk when the first big shells fell in that quaint city. Somehow or other he got to the eastern battle front and from there he sent an interview with Von Hindenburg. Astonishingly, he was in London when the Lusitania was sunk; and yet he was one of the few correspondents who saw the French advance near Arras.

During those early stages of the war he must have performed prodigies of travel, of battle with censors, of writing well under trying conditions, and of risking his idiotic neck. We did not think much about it at the time, but now when I run through a scrap-book of Sinful Goode's cables I am astonished.

The Old Man, meantime, made no secret of his delight in the work of "our own correspondent." He used to say: "Best inspiration I ever had, sending that chap to the war. Of course, he'll get killed, but—fortunes of the profession, you know."

Goode did not get killed. Instead, he got bored. When the western front settled down to its deadlock in the trenches Goode became silent, and probably sulky. There were long weeks when he sent nothing. It was even rumored that he was coming home. The Gallipoli campaign, however, restored him. I don't recall how it was he got there, if we ever knew; but suddenly he was heard from in a dispatch that proved to be his first blunder. He cabled us that the British landings had succeeded, and that the capture of the peninsula was certain. I remember well the flurry in the office that day; the telegraph editor rushing in to the Old Man with Goode's cable, and rushing out again red in the face; also, later, how a dubious conference developed the fact that the Associated Press did not support Sinful's story, and how the Old Man said: "I don't care. I stick by Goode. What's the use of having a special correspondent if you don't believe him?" We kept up the eight-column head, and kept up our spirits by talking about the censor.

It all seemed so exciting then, and now seems so dead!

Well, we rushed a "query" by cable, and after about a week we began to wonder if the Old Man would recall our friend Sinful. Whether he considered this we never learned; but evidently he could not have done it if he had tried. Young-Man-Going-Somewhere had always just gone somewhere else before messages of that kind arrived. And by the time it had become fully clear that Constantinople was not to be captured Goode was up in the Balkans.

Does it seem incredible that a correspondent—especially one working for the Old Man—should dodge about so independent of office orders? Well, if it does, I can only say that Sinful Goode was *sui generis*, that he followed no traditions, and that he would not have obeyed orders if he had

had them. The Old Man was wise enough not to send him any.

The Old Man would never, for example, have ordered Sinful Goode to join the Serbian army on its great retreat. Goode sent himself on that assignment. Pursuing his faculty of getting "in" with big people, he attached himself to the personal headquarters of Prince Alexander—called the prince by his first name, probably—and went clear through to the coast with that valiant group leading a stream of ragged, desperate men. Goode slept on the frozen ground along with the prince and his army; starved with them; fought their battles against marauding bands, and helped save the remnants. At the coast he separated from the army, took a rowboat out into the Adriatic and caught some kind of tramp steamer, whereon he made a long and hideous journey to Athens. Arriving there, a very skeleton of the ruddy and cheerful Sinful Goode, he dictated ten thousand words, and then collapsed.

When the Old Man received that cable, he sent Goode the single word: "Congratulations."

This was the answer:

"Congratulations received. After a man has had all the infernal starvation tours of the war and has been the goat for the toughest assignments and got nothing out of it but dysentery it feels great to get a boost like yours, that cost such tolls—oh, yes, I assure you it does! How about that salary raise? How about that request for 5,000 French francs I never got? Does anybody ever think about me? Does office know I'm alive? Just received copies paper see my Balkan stuff butchered and stuck on inside pages. Nice work, thank you. Congratulations.

"GOODE."

He was so angry, you see, that he put in a lot of "thes" and "ands," at commercial rate.

The Old Man, looking grieved, brought in the message to the city editor, and remarked: "I don't know what to do with that fellow."

The city editor pondered, and together they concocted this:

"Goode, Athens: Do you want to come home?"

But Sinful never got this message, for he had started for Paris, there to squander huge amounts of the Press funds in peach Melbas at Amenonville, and raspberry tarts at Paillard's and "American cocktails" at the Chatham.

[IV]

IT would hardly be worth while to describe in so much detail the rest of Sinful's war experience. He got into Russia right after the first revolution, and got out again in time to see the vanguard of the American troops land in France. Later in the year he returned to Russia, where he made friends with the bolsheviki and had three meals a day quite regularly. He was here, there and everywhere during the next year; had typhus in Warsaw, got part of an ear clipped off near St. Mihiel, and fought a duel with a French editor. He was growing restless and homesick, that was evident. We began to get post-cards from him begging for news of the staff. He sent Josslyn the latest book by Barbusse, and wrote: "For God's sake, try to smuggle some American cigars to me." Then—the armistice. And a cable from Goode: "Sailing Thursday Adriatic." I fancy the Old Man breathed a luxurious sigh.

Among the staff there was both glee and incertitude over the approaching return of the Great Correspondent. Would Goodey (as we had taken to calling him) show signs of being "up-stage"? Was it possible for this distinguished journalist, who had been consorting with princes, generals, premiers and proprietors of Parisian cafes to meet us on our level? Would he overwhelm us with French and Italian? Would he be wearing spats and a fur-collared overcoat?

These mild anxieties we kept mostly to ourselves; only it was said more than once, with a certain disgust, "He'll think he's too good for ordinary news work."

After about a week the signs of his approach began to accumulate. A letter or two with foreign post-marks, addressed "John Temple Goode, Esq."

Telephone message from prominent citizens, asking when Mr. Goode might be expected. Then a telegram from Sinful himself: "Arriving Saturday noon be ready to develop first photos armistice celebration Paris."

About one o'clock Saturday a group of us sitting in the cigar store saw passing a tallish, square-shouldered figure surmounted by a weather-stained fedora and slung about with a camera. It was Goode, God bless him! The same ruddy, challenging face; the same old mangled cigar between his teeth. Even the same suit of clothes he wore to Mexico, I shouldn't wonder.

Forgetting his greatness, we rushed out into the street, shook him and slapped him; and we said, "Sinful, you old egg!" and we cried, "You big stiff, you're looking fine—but you're getting grey."

And the friend of princes grinned and spat, and then said: "Look here, fellows, I've got some photos to get developed. Got a story to write, too. Gosh, but the old loop looks great. How's the Old Man? How's Josslyn? How's everybody?"

In fifteen minutes he was in the Old Man's room arguing about his expense account; and we knew that Sinful Goode had returned unchanged.

[V]

HE is unchanged still.
It is now some years since the war. Everybody, including Goode, has almost forgotten it.

He has been away twice, the first time in South America, the second in Siberia. On both trips he worked like fury, "kicked" continually by cable, lived among outlandish folk and took insane risks; only to return unchanged.

He attends luncheons given by bankers, to obtain his opinion of possibilities of foreign trade. He receives mysterious letters from the State Department, desiring information. He makes addresses before chambers of commerce. Three publishing houses have asked him for books, but he has been too lazy to write them, and he has never been able to finish his novel.

Sometimes when I see him pondering at his desk I suspect he finds greater futility in life than any of us. He has never had a home. During his frantic dashes about the world he has accumulated nothing but a crazy-quilt of baggage labels and a collection of room keys. His wife—did I mention that he has a wife?—has seen him only about three weeks of each year; her life has been a procession of *pensions*. Goode has saved nothing; he owns nothing, save a helter-skelter collection of pipes, Prussian helmets, Japanese fans, autographs, and time tables.

Ah, but he has his friendships! Like the rest of us, he has these, though all else may have failed. Indeed, he has a home. This is it, this news-room, with its battered desks and its cracked plastering. Here, amid the happy family—the

Star, Josslyn, Brown, the city editor, amiable Barlow and others—he sinks into a contented comradeship that is faintly like drawing up to a table full of brothers and sisters.

Then there is the cigar store. Sinful Goode sits smoking a mangled cigar, and grinning at each of us in turn.

"Say, Goodey, why don't you write those books and get famous?"

"Yes, Goodey, why don't you capitalize your name?"

"My name? It stands for fried fish, I guess. Write books! I'm a newspaper guy, I am. So long's I get my stuff in the paper . . . ."

A pause.

"What are Russian hotels like? Do they heat 'em?"

Goode yawns.

"Say, when did they start the new Madison street bridge?" he inquires with real interest.

There is nothing to be got out of him.

[VI]

IT almost seems as though he might stay at home now.

But no. He confides that this very afternoon he is going to "talk turkey to the old man," and tell him he has a chance to go to the polar regions in an aeroplane, and shall he try it on?

Until he is silver-haired and palsied, and until

his fingers can no longer pound a portable typewriter, he will always be the Young-Man-Going-Somewhere.

{VI}

The Cub

[I]

IF wishes were horses, the Cub would ride long, dusty trails with Sinful Goode. As it is, he sits much of the time with his feet on his desk, and his hands in his pockets, and his head sunken upon his breast, and dreams.

He is not asleep; not quite. Therefore his dreams are not of fantasy, but of probability. They are ambitions. They are his present life a thousand times glorified and decorated. But they are as futile as any dreams; and when they are over they are just as bitter.

The Cub half slumbers at his desk, while far down the room a group of "executives," transcendent beings to whom the Cub says "sir," discuss matters in general and occasionally, catching sight of the Cub, discuss him. These voices are inaudible to the Cub. Could he hear them they would make a strange accompaniment to his dreams, much as the distant and irrelevant remarks made by doctors and nurses sound to a patient half-way under an anaesthetic.

This is an antiphony of the Cub's illusions and the "executives'" voices.

[II]

IT should be noted that the Cub has been here only a fortnight. He was recommended to the city editor by the advertising manager, who learned of him through a big advertiser who has a great friend whose son the Cub is.

A voice: "Of course, I don't usually fall for these fish that get in by way of business office. But I'm the chief sufferer, after all."

Second voice: "No, you're wrong; I am."

Third voice (to first): "We know you, George. You're as soft as the advertising manager, and the two of you together, if it wasn't for the Old Man, would soon have the shop full of Oxfordmen and lap-dogs."

First voice: "You chaps go to hell. As for this Cub, I think he's got the makin's."

A new voice: "I think so, too."

Third voice: "Oh, as for you, Josslyn, if you found a sow's ear on the sidewalk you'd advertise it in the Lost and Found."

Et seq.

[III]

HE dreams.

At last he is a journalist. Behold, he is here, surrounded by great news-men and great writers; he is sitting, as by right, in this chamber of fascinating shadows. Only a little while ago he walked in for the first time, passing the door-boy loftily because he had a *right* to come in. He remembers other doors and other door-boys; remembers them with pain and with disdain. He recalls pacing various corridors, while his card, inscribed "Frederick Reid Dunstane," went with his soul into the invisible. Now all that is over. He is "in."

In the dream he is a larger, more dignified, more intellectual being than formerly. During those waits in various corridors he was a puny and forlorn soul, a lip-biter, a waif quite without standing or importance. He forgot that he was a member of select college organizations, a tea-fighter of prowess, a superb figure on the dance-floor, and a D. S. M. As he stood in those corridors, leaning sullenly against the wall, he eyed the light-hearted, fraternizing young men, plainly members of the staff, who passed into the elevator and who gave him glances he considered mocking; and no shivering Lazarus ever eyed banquet guests more humbly or more enviously than he. But now he is grown once more to fill out his clothes, and he carries a cane at the same angle as the Star's cane, and he has already lent five dollars to the Drunkard, and he calls the city editor half-familiarly "boss." Also he reads the paper's editorials scornfully, as is the news-room habit, and he has learned to speak of contemporary publications as loutish and unenterprising.

In his dreams he is already quite the equal of his mates in resource of undertaking and in savoir-faire; and he feels more than competent stylistically. He is, in fact, bursting with literary impulse. Original phrases are spurting within him. (He does not dream that they were suggested to him by the Star's latest story.) In fancy he opens his typewriter and writes. He writes furiously, fluently, in an ecstasy. And boys in relays stand at his elbow, seizing the sheets as they pour from the machine. And the city editor strolls up behind him and says, affectionately: "Take it easy, old chap; you've got fifteen minutes yet." Then the presses thunder more loudly, and behold, here is his story, long, black, and lovely, on the first page. And there are groups of great journalists about, devouring his story. All the copy-readers are talking about it.

What figure is this, marching in through the swinging door, and crying out, "Who wrote this splendid story?"

"Why, it is the Old Man, who somehow has overlooked the Cub's presence hitherto, but who now seeks him out with a warm grip of the hand, and the tribute, "You are the sort of material we need."

[IV]

FIRST voice: "The reason is that if I gave him more than two sticks to write he'd murder it."

Second voice: "Yes, they're all alike, those cubs. If old Rud Kipling himself were to tackle a good, snappy fire his story would have to be rewritten."

Third voice: "I read his copy yesterday. Lord, it was fierce!"

A new voice: "Oh, he'll catch on. I was talking to him this morning . . . ."

All the previous voices: "Josslyn, when will you learn?"

[V]

HE is dreaming about being called out of bed at six a. m. and sent to take charge of a special crew assigned to cover the city's greatest fire.

The taxicab tears westward over the river, toward the typhoon of smoke and flame. The Cub is sternly calm. To one of his three companions he says: "You, Billy, you'd better get the list of firms and losses"; to another, "Murray, you are assigned to dead and injured"; he directs the third, "Wallace, do features. I'll go on ahead with the chief, up into the building." He pulls up his overcoat collar. "Report to me in half an hour.

I'll take your stuff into the office and write the story."

They arrive at the fire. The great reporter, formerly the Cub, descries the fire chief, a massive figure in rubber coat, peering up at the tall streams of water and piercing the steam-clouds with his old eyes.

"Hello, chief; I'm Dunstane, of the Press."

"Why, hello, Dunstane; glad you're here."

The inside facts of the fire are immediately in the Cub's possession. He rushes on, on, quite to the foremost skirmish line of the battle. He climbs with a group of pipemen to an upper floor, swirling with smoke, and with its windows yawning empty to the sky. In this deserted loft he discovers a telephone. Good! The wire is working. He connects the office—it is now seven o'clock— and calls the city desk, calmly and sternly.

"Mr. Brown? I'm up in the burning building, cut off from rescue, if anything should happen. . . . No, I think there is no real danger. Those crashes you hear are only falling bricks. . . . Give you the complete story in half an hour. Ta-ta!"

He drops from the window in safety. He brushes aside anxious firemen who would give him first aid. Though bruised and half choked, he rounds up his crew, receives their reports, and taxis back to the office, where he curtly announces: "Two million loss; gimme some copy-paper quick."

The staff watch him with awe. From a far corner a Cub—oh, a much more verdant and ineffective Cub than Dunstane once was—projects himself into the dream, steals up and eyes Dunstane's flying fingers. And afterward Dunstane kindly allows the Cub to speak to him, and he tells how he did it. And the Cub accepts a cigar——

[VI]

A VOICE: "He was out with Wallace the other day on that 4-11 alarm. Wallace says he kicked the whole time because we weren't going to let him write anything. Got several of his figures wrong, too. I wonder if it's any use. . . ."

Second voice: "Oh, he must have got some good experience out of it."

Third voice: "He ought to have plenty of nerve. I'm told he brought down three German planes in the Argonne."

First voice: "But look at him over there, half-asleep. What do you suppose he's day-dreaming about?"

[VII]

THIS time it is about Europe. Europe, where he once was. How he hated it! With what zest he enjoyed everything which read, looked or smelled like America. Ah, if he ever got back to God's country, why, never again!

But now, if he could only get back to Europe!

He would make a distinguished Paris correspondent, he would, what with his knowledge of French. Would they let him try it? Why, the cables he would send would place the Press on a new basis, internationally speaking. He could go tomorrow—tomorrow, and start in at once interviewing monarchs and presidents. In this vision he has passed far beyond the level of that grimy being of a moment ago, condescending to talk to fire chiefs. He now has the entree to intellectual salons and to grave council chambers. He has no need to make appointments with premiers and those fellows; but immediately he sends in his card, "Frederick Reid Dunstane," obsequious secretaries usher him into gilded bureaus of the most high, and he confers—he does not interview, he confers—with the men who are making a new Europe.

There is no present hope, perhaps. But wait—wait! They will find him out. They are bound to realize soon that he is the very man for the Paris post. Preferably Paris, but as a second choice, London. The dream sweeps on. A war breaks out. He is the first correspondent to be informed of the ultimatum. He rushes to the cable office, and barriers of censorship are officially lifted, that the great Frederick Dunstane may send the TRUTH.

The President of the United States cables to Mr. Dunstane to learn further details. Mr. Dunstane advises intervention by the United States.

And all this is chronicled in the Press as the work of "our correspondent."

In the evening Mr. Dunstane repairs to the Cafe Napolitain, on the Boulevard des Capucines, where all the great correspondents meet to sip brandy, and where all the *monde,* together with no small part of the *demi-monde,* sit at small tables and gaze at celebrities. Mr. Dunstane appears, great but modest. Groups of drinkers spring up to offer him their chairs, or to grasp his hand, or to demand the latest inside news. He is unaffected by his distinction, speaks democratically to the correspondents of the Times and the Morning Telegraph, accepts one of the proffered chairs, and sips brandy—very abstemiously. The great city, the great world, in whose center he sits and of which, in fact, he is the center, gyrates around him. And he, breaker of nations, but still a journalist, takes his ease.

[VIII]

A VOICE: "You know the first day he came he asked if there wasn't a job open in Paris."
Laughter.

[IX]

THE news room seems to be emptying for the day. The group of "executives" has scattered, all save the city editor. He is folding up his copies of the late editions, and pinning discarded stuff on spindles, preparatory to closing his desk.

The mysterious shadows of the long, gloomy room are deepening. And the Cub is rousing from his visions.

But not before he sees himself grey, portly and whiskered, as it is possible some day he may be. Yes, he can prefigure even that far-away time. And what will he be then? Well, surely an owner, nothing else. He will be a cultured, traveled, urbane owner, sitting at a polished mahogany desk entirely clear of papers, and conducting business over a battery of telephones. He will wear a frock coat with silk lapels, and be spoken of for senator. He will be too busy, probably, to do any actual editorial work, but he will have many, many able men to do this for him; and they will know that although his writing days are over, he was once the best of them all, and still possesses such professional acuteness that "it's no use trying to put anything over on the old man."

He will have a new building, instead of this modest structure from which the Press is issued. It will have a tower, and a huge clock with a luminous face, and there will be letters in blazing electricity all around the cornice: "The Press; Frederick Reid Dunstane, Proprietor." On an election night his portrait, as the man who chose the new President of the United States, will be displayed in red fire.

But he will remain democratic. He will invite his editors to lunch, and know his printers by their first names. Yes, even the newest and homeliest of the copy-boys shall have access to him.

[X]

THERE is a shuffling of feet beside the Cub's desk. A grimy paw musses the papers on the desk. A voice of adolescence speaks in rather execrable accents:

"Say, Mr. Brown says you should finish that club notice for tomorrow's paper. He says you should hurry."

The Cub slowly removes his feet from his desk, takes his hands from his pockets, and blinks.

In the full light of reason he perceives the blunt truth: He is but one rung higher than the copy-boy.

{VII}
The Old Man

[1]

IN these days it seems incredible that the Old Man was ever a Cub. Yet such he was. I have seen a photograph of him at the age of twenty. There looks out from the frame a lean, eager face, with wide eyes and sensitive lips. A startling brush of hair, a la pompadour, crowns the forehead. The personality that quivers there is vivid despite the fading of the print. It looks wistfully and severely down the years, and offers silent criticism of the bulkier personality that it has become.

The Old Man now confesses "fifty odd." His hair crosses his skull in sparse, grey-black strands. His blue eyes smolder behind heavy spectacles. His shoulders, his hands, his limbs, his walk, have become ponderous. The floor creaks when he traverses it. His chair groans at his touch. The weight of his responsibility is upon him and all that he does; and the weight of his authority is upon us. We are now the lean, eager creatures straining at life. The Old Man has become a figure of another generation and another significance. He symbolizes government, importance and permanence. He is our law-giver, our repressor; but he is also our security, our refuge. Who shall chastise us? The Old Man. But who shall restore and comfort us? None but the Old Man. He sits there supporting "the office" upon his broad shoulders, suggesting in his formidable physique itself that the institution we belong to is no fragile thing. To be able to do this has cost him something; it has cost him the ardency and sensitiveness of the photograph. All of that is grown over by the protective layers, both physical and mental, that he has had to build up. It is grown over—but perhaps it still lives.

[II]

PROMPTLY on the stroke of eight in the morning the Old Man emerges from the elevator, and a minute later one can hear the lid of his private desk go up with a rush and crash. The swivel chair gives its familiar groan. There is a moment's silence, and then the Old Man's voice is heard, calling for the morning papers.

His voice is a curious organ, musical with chest tones, but sharpening easily to acrimony, and sometimes, in extreme impatience, becoming plaintive, despairing. At this hour of the day, when the boy, as usual, has forgotten the morning papers, the Old Man's voice is always at its highest note of weary insolence. In the few words it utters, it suggests the immense distance between the Old Man and the boy, and the utter triviality of the process of discharging the boy. But, somehow, the Old Man never does discharge the boy. The small, round face of this functionary reflects surprise, fear and enormous stupidity as he peers in at the Old Man's door. He sums up everything with his "Yessir."

"Tell Brown to come here," commands the Old Man, with an impatient jounce in his chair.

Brown arrives, in shirt-sleeves and eye-shade. His lean face is apprehensive, but his chin is determined, and there is a twist of something like humor about his mouth. He stands silently in the door, with his hands in his pockets.

The Old Man pretends to be busy reading a letter. At length he slowly turns his fearsome spectacles, through which his eyes appear magnified and very bright, in Brown's direction, and he emits a slight sound, unrecognizable either as greeting or as warning. A pause, and he says:

"We muffed that jewel robbery story yesterday. The Journal had it all over us."

Another pause.

"The Journal always beats us on a police story." This rouses Brown, as is the intention.

"Not always," he says quietly.

The Old Man brings down his hand upon his letters.

"Yes—always. When I say always, I mean—always. Yesterday, today, and forever. Our police staff is no good. It needs a shaking up—nothing's ever done unless I start it myself." The chair groans. "Here I am, twenty years older than any of you, and I have to furnish the ginger. You young fellows . . ." another untranslatable sound.

Brown is paler than before.

"Maybe you think," he counters in his thin, steady voice, "maybe you thing the staff shake-up should begin at the top."

"Maybe it should," retorts the Old Man instantly. He always rises to a challenge of this sort. The two men eye each other. Outside in the hall the boy is telegraphing to other boys that hell is popping.

"Well," says Brown, taking his hands out of his pockets, "I've done my best."

"All I can say to that," blurts the Old Man, with his habitual answer to the plea he has heard a thousand times, "is that your best isn't good enough."

"Very well," says the city editor, taking off his eye-shade, as though by the act he lays down office; "very well, then, I . . ."

At this moment the telephone on the Old Man's desk rings. Compressing his lips, he takes up the receiver and listens, his cold blue gaze resting absently upon Brown. He speaks shortly once, and hangs up.

"Look here," he remarks, quite in his ordinary tone, "there's going to be a riot on the Board of Trade this morning. Better start somebody down early." He speaks now on terms of equality and complete friendliness. "The situation has been cooking up for some time. You'd better have Manlius go down and help out Riggs. It'll be some story."

"It may be the big line for the second mail," suggests Brown, brightening up. "I'll write that head myself. I'll . . ."

"Go and start something. Get out of here while I read my mail. Scat!"

The incident is closed. The day has started right. Both the Old Man and Brown, stimulated by their tiff and reconciliation, plunge into work with vim and zest. An hour later, the Old Man, having run through his mail, clipped out three suggestions for editorials, delivered various orders to the composing room and elsewhere, telegraphed instructions to New York and Washington correspondents, and disposed of a politician concerned about the "injudicious policy of our leading afternoon paper," strolls into the news-room for a look around. Brown's razor back is bent over a mass of proofs.

"Don't strain your eyes, my boy," says the Old Man, pausing beside him; "you need a better light here."

He passes on, past the copy-readers, crabbedly disposing of their work, past the bench-full of small boys, who look demurely downcast as he passes and scowl terribly behind his back, and on among the desks of the reporters. He halts at a desk in a corner. The occupant instantly stops typewriting, and rises.

"How's Fosket?" asks the Old Man. "Were you out at the hospital last night?"

There is reassurance about the appendix of Fosket, and the reporter is left to his work. The Old Man wanders on, arriving at the row of windows that overlook the street. In the street is the usual daily swarm of trucks, taxis, pedestrians, thronging by under the jagged level of the elevated railroad. It is a grim perspective. It is a segment of the city ridden by mechanisms, ridden by routine, by desperate errands. Here at its vortex the city is harsh, dour, fearfully in a hurry. It sends up a voice, an influence, into this newspaper office! it sends up messages of the conflict, the confusion, of its forty-eight nationalities and its forty-eight thousand ambitions. Anything may happen here. There may be at any moment an outbreak of crime committed in a blunt, dauntless manner rivaling the Mexican border. There may be accident, swift and hideous. There may be some less overt but quite as startling manifestation of the intricate, violent, dazzlingly vital city.

The Old Man sniffs the air, loving this city of his. He is for the moment deaf to what is behind his back; he is in an interlude, forgetting his desk and all that is upon it. He gazes down critically, masterfully, with an appearance of premonition, into the familiar street. And there is about him almost a kind of majesty, because of his power of impressing himself upon this multitude, and because of the air of the patrician that hangs always about him.

For the Old Man was not born of this swarm. He was thrust into his present environment and his present tasks, partly by destiny, partly by his own complex nature.

His full name (only a few of us know this) is Norbert William DeLancy Thain. He signs himself "N. W. Thain."

[III]

A FEW years ago a dispatch announced the death of a wealthy maiden lady named Thain. She was said to be "almost the last survivor of a distinguished eastern family." There were hints about rich acres on Long Island, about libraries full of old masters, and the like. Soon after the dispatch was published the Old Man was absent for a few days, and it was rumored that he had gone east. The rumor subsided upon his return, and the very, very faint conjecture that he was a connection of the baronial Miss Thain was speedily forgotten.

But the fact, which a few of us know, is that the Old Man was her brother. It is not difficult to fill in the outlines of the story. Indeed, the Old Man, in his rare moments of reminiscence, has supplied all that was needed.

Why, then, is he not at this moment living as a country gentleman on Long Island, buying and selling racing stables, and occasionally scaring Wall street into fits, instead of inviting soul devastation by managing a newspaper? The answer revolves around a mystery not peculiar to The Mysterious Profession, but common to all; the mystery of a young man's ambition, the thing that "sends them into it." Norbert William DeLancy Thain did not wish to be a country gentleman. He did want to be a newspaper man. Perhaps he wanted as well to be a writer—a novelist or a poet. We do not know this. In these days he speaks with profound disdain of novelists and poets. But he himself has told us that he was determined to be a newspaper man. He—yes, I am sure he said this—he "gave up everything for it." So we have a pretty reliable picture of him engaging in a stormy argument with his father, then declaring his independence and joining the motley company, half genius and half charlatan, then common along Park Row. He has told us about Park Row, with the slight hyperbole that tinges his reminiscences. Sometimes he has declared that he belonged to a golden age of journalism, when enterprise reached its zenith, and the pursuit of a "beat" recked no cost, and that of this golden age he himself was one of the most luminous figures. At other times he has satirized both Park Row and his younger self, and assured us that we ourselves belonged to "the greatest newspaper in history." But it remains certain that he was a reporter in New York, and eventually a writer much prized. Was it not he who as a mere boy "covered" the rush to settle Oklahoma, the great Chicago railway strike, and the Santiago campaign? It was. He has told us so, and has shown us the scar on his neck made by a Spanish bullet. The Old Man has given us details of these things during the long hours of waiting for a court verdict or a strike settlement. Expansive hours, these, when more than one department chief 'reminisced," and we youngsters hung about, fascinated.

But there is very little to show at what period the Old Man gave up star reporting for desk work, or to tell us why he did it. We can only surmise; we can only apply to his case the things that govern most newspaper careers and assume that, having committed himself to the hazards of the profession, he was forced to accept his destiny. This destiny usually assumes one of two forms: either the acceptance of high responsibility, together with crushing worry and deadening routine, or a decadence from the position of Star to one of shabby obscurity. It was impossible for a man of the Old Man's temper to take the slide to the level of "once a great reporter." One day it became inevitable for him to be an executive and thus to exert the acuteness, the immense energy, the professional wisdom, that had come with his years.

But on that day, mind you, he laid aside forever the delight of "seeing himself in print." He forfeited his literary creative powers. He parted with a section of his individuality. It is all very well to say that his imaginative gifts now figure on every page of the paper, that he "expresses himself through others," and so on. All very well, but every time such words are spoken of a man born a literary artist, they utter a requiem. The funeral of the Old Man as a writer has now been held so often that every one supposes him to be used to it. But is he? Does not there persist in him, will there not persist to his death day, the strange, bitter-sweet egoism that will not be satisfied without "seeing one's-self in print"?

Sometimes—rarely—the Old Man dictates an editorial, or perhaps a few lines of flourish at the beginning of an important news story. There is in these fragments a deadly acid quality, or more often a felicitous turn of phrase, that shows what power still smolders in the Old Man's spirit. It is revealed further by his treatment of us, by his disdain for crude, hackneyed expression, by his delight in a piece of writing that has original color, by his tenderness toward the sensitive gropers among us.

He comes out of his room sometimes, grasping the latest issue in both hands, and with his eyes blazing.

"Who wrote this?" he demands. "By G——, it's good!"

And he returns to his lair, satisfied with the outburst, without waiting for an answer to his question.

Or it may be that he finds in a rival paper a story that rises above mediocrity, that has a note of "the real thing." He will rave for half an hour about the ability of this anonymous literary rival. And we hang our heads.

Meantime, although it is so plain that the Old Man is at heart an artist, and that he loves excellent writing with the consuming love others have for music, we never think of him as a writer at all; that is, we know what he could do, but we never expect him to do it. There he is in his niche, a huge and conspicuous niche, with a sign over him "Executive." Oh, yes, he could and did do things; he was an artist once; but not now. Now he is the Boss—a being of whom to ask questions or from whom to receive maledictions, a being who controls pay-rolls. He is stage-director and prompter. Someone else speaks the parts and receives the curtain calls.

All of this constitutes a sort of tragedy.

[IV]

THERE can be no doubt that the Old Man has a plural nature. "Dual" seems scarcely to be the word.

Two of his selves are the artist and the executive. The executive, when that phase of DeLancy Thain's life opened, rose into preponderance over the artist very easily; and as time went on his increasing virility and love of conflict demanded more and more a tempestuous field. Perhaps from the first he instinctively sought trouble, as the saying is. It is certain that in this city which I have characterized as intricate and violent he is at home. The fact, to some extent, mitigates the tragedy of the suppressed artist.

A newspaper with the breath of life in it is ever on the offensive. Its hates stream out to "Little Hell," "The Valley," and the Gashouse District," breathing challenge to bad men whereever they hide. Even if there be no battle for the time being with crooks and gangsters there is conflict with somebody. To be the leader in this amiable business of making enemies requires a big fist and a blunt answer. It involves the Old Man from time to time in clashes—usually verbal—with uncouth persons in whom somehow or other there was born a devil both fierce and canny. This is no place for a lily-fingered, lisping individual. The Old Man has to be prepared, and is, to oppose to brutal, foul speech a resistance quite as brutal, though perhaps not as foul. He casts off, almost daily, his hereditary cloak of the patrician and "mixes it" with jail-bird sons of jail-birds. He is a match—he who might have spent his afternoons at tea dances at the Ritz-Carleton—for any of the products of this city that includes in its composite soul the low instincts of a dozen races.

When his telephone bell rings there may come to him the voice of a six-foot gangster announcing, "You —— ——, I'm comin' around there today to beat your block off."

And the Old Man must be prepared to answer the gangster at once, and not in French, either.

There are conflicts of a more diplomatic sort; political struggles, or controversies involving even women and scholars. The Old Man has mastered the weapons of these as well. The point with him is, never to yield. On no account does the Old Man give ground. There are times when it suits him to revert to the patrician, and then it is a delightful experience to hear him suavely, perhaps ironically, dispose of the opposition. It is even more delicious to see him plume himself after the encounter; to observe how his whole personality glistens with the consciousness that neither in breeding nor in intellect does he concede an atom to these persons who speak with the accents of Harvard and of Vassar.

He is equipped, too, with every art needed to cope with the disputes that come up in the office. To us he is capable of being blunt or suave, persuasive or sarcastic, as the nature of the tangle requires. He is death upon the frequent situation in which two minor executives come to him with "I can't go on working here if Wade does," and vice versa. He merely says: "You may both quit, then." Equally fatal is he to the youth who complains that "credit" is being subtracted from him. The Old Man sweetly and in the purest English subtracts the rest of the credit.

It is we, of course, who see the Old Man in all his moods, who have learned that his nature is really plural. We see him morose, joyous, tender, abusive, frivolous, weary. We see him uplifted in one of those gorgeous moments of great news which come so rarely; and we see him grimly assailed by routine, bored to death, but hanging on. Sometimes he suggests to us a hollow, hopeless soul, sucked dry of enthusiasm or initiative. An hour later, and he may be leading us with the fury of a youth; or, coatless at the "stone," singing over his proofs and slapping printers on the back.

There are days when he seems to hate us all. There are days when his affection enfolds us like sunshine.

He is brief with the Cub, sardonic with Sinful Goode, amiable and savage by turns with the Star, majestic with the Drunkard, and strictly on his good behavior with Josslyn. There must be a story about his relations with Josslyn, "the old-timer." We shall have to look into it before we finish.

[V]

IN this haphazard world of ours, so easily upset by a word, by a false touch or an unprofessional act, the Old Man is the symbol of permanence. That powerful body seems never to weaken, that mind returns every morning to the challenge, to the battle, to the semi-paternal care of us all.

Ten years hence, how will it be? Surely by that time he will have begun to weaken. And with what memories can he mitigate the distress of age. To what can he point with the words, "I made this"? For the record of his days will be the hundreds of trivial thoughts and motions spent upon "getting out the paper"; the lavishing of immense zeal upon an evanescent product, forgotten as soon as made.

Perhaps, when the false fires are quenched, there will be nothing for him to rejoice over—nothing but us. There will remain among the ashes of his public and his enterprises only us, his children, his disciples. Perhaps we shall have become, in our turn, weighty, authoritative persons, who can "get out a paper." He will have bequeathed his life to us, and we shall bequeath it again to vivid youths like the one pictured in the Old Man's photograph.

{VIII}

The Poet

[I]

ENTLEMEN, should you meet a stalwart person walking the streets bareheaded and glowing with mysterious ecstasy, will you kindly bring him back to the office? That is our Poet. The Old Man would like to see him.

It is a whim of the Old Man's, and of nobody else, that we shall employ a poet to write critical articles. An incongruity, surely; what do you think? Are not critics supposed to be bloodless, blue-nosed persons, pedantic, prudent, prim, and accurate on the typewriter? And do they not punch clocks faithfully? Poets never punch clocks.

There is a disposition in our office, however, to forgive the Old Man his eccentricity; to love him the more because he employs The Poet. Beyond doubt, the presence of The Poet lends color to this pasture wherein we dig post-holes and hunt mares-nests. It is certain that our days would be gloomier were it not for the leisurely, genial, enigmatic being who moves about among the shades. To find him at one's elbow, quite unexpectedly, furnishes a moment of novelty and of warmth. To hear him boom: "Some first page today—man, that's journalism!" is almost as forceful praise as a note from the Owner. Besides this, it does us good to gather around his desk and hear him talk. There is nearly always—at least, during The Poet's variable "office hours," there is usually a knot of young reporters listening to his wisdom. And it sometimes makes the Old Man nervous when he comes in and finds work at a standstill. But the Old Man knows he is chiefly to blame, so he smiles secretly and goes away.

The Old Man is wont to boast: "I've managed to keep that man on my staff for five years without a break."

A rightful boast. It is no joke to keep a poet anywhere.

[II]

HE has been here five years. He has been happy, we think. As for us, we have seen poems born. We have watched The Poet at his window, lounging deep in his chair, his powerful hands knotted, his dark, rugged face locked in a solemn dream. The poems themselves have been on exhibition at various stages: as pencilled yellow slips, as clean sheets re-typed for the printer, as long rolls of galley-proofs. We have seen poems fresh from the shell, shivering in a philistine world; and we have seen them again, months later, fricaseed in books, or set forth with professorial comment, or translated into French and Italian and Spanish. All this makes The Poet more incongruous than ever. Who is he, after all? A great man, or only one of us? One cannot doubt that he travels in an orbit that often takes him very far away, and that at his perihelion he is quite beyond our vision. Yet he returns as regularly as he goes, and when he is again within our range, and when the flight of gaudy and tawdry events does not engross us too much, he is as actual as Barlow, and as vivid as The Star. In these returns to earth he shares the office dramas. He is one of the first to be told of a big scoop, a grievous quarrel, or a new baby. He is interested in the people of the news-room; and he has periods of absorption in news itself.

Sitting in his deep old chair he may preach to us like this:

"You and I are artists; you as much as I. They call newspaper work a trade, or a profession. More often it is an art. . . . Besides writing, there is staging the effect. Dramatists do that; so do newspaper men. Dramatists set a stage; newspaper men, dealing with a great event, give a setting of type and a proper bally-hoo. . . . The novelist has his 'control,'—character; the painter has his—beauty. The newspaperman has his 'control'—news. What is news? It is what interests everybody. How do we know it interests everybody? Why, we simply know . . ." etc., etc.

[III]

OR IN the cigar store he may suddenly appear among the clouds of smoke, with a long, loose-rolled stogie in his lips, and argue about the current murder trial. And then, quite as though he were no more august than the Cub, he may say: "Who's for a cup of Java?"

Or on an election night he may saunter in between the littered desks and inquire: "How's Diamond Joe running?"

But for all this, we know that he is an extraneous spirit, who dwells among us, yet apart. He travels in mysterious spaces beyond our tired vision. He is the office mystery, just as the Drunkard is its bad boy, and Josslyn its Sir Philip Sidney. He has another life somewhere; perhaps in his country cottage, where through an attic window he drinks star-light. We can't tell just why the world makes so much of him. Some of us shake our heads over his poetry, and say "I can't make sense of it." Or we ask The Poet what it means, and he replies, "God knows."

Can't we get at our mystery somehow, can't we solve him?

Suppose that we step outside of the news-room, just for once, and follow him to the antipodes; to the other side of the orbit. Let's assemble the crowd; make it a night off. Tomorrow the news-room again, the detestable clock, the insane telephones, the petty conflicts. Tonight, The Poet.

[IV]

EIGHT steps down from the level of the glossy boulevard. Two steps to the right into the restaurant with red chairs and green walls. This is the place. The red chairs stand in semi-circles before a fire-place, and on the mantel-shelf there are plaster statuettes, and Quimper plates, and this and that. All very chic. It is not a restaurant this evening; it is a setting for The Poet. But what a setting! Think of him among the statuettes and the tall candles, the cages of imitation parrots, the walls frescoed with pink flower-baskets. Our poet! May he step softly amid this porcelain.

The red chairs gradually fill up. From the boulevard swept by snow squalls and by streaks of motor-lights people are blowing in. We, the news-room "crowd," blow in and are dumfounded to find there are no seats for us. The place is packed. "Everybody" is here: The cognoscenti, and the literati, and the younger intellectuals and the neo-Bohemians and the academics, and the iconoclasts and the abracadabrists. Everybody who writes, or writes about writings or knows people who talk about those who write about writing. The serene small editress of a magazine enters, and five young poets jump up to offer her their places. A literary critic appears in the doorway, leading an abashed-looking trio of suburban friends. In a corner glowers a group of long-haired youths with horn spectacles and scornful conversation. An old man, white bearded, is squeezed between two bobbed-haired screechers. Sophomores and sub-debs arrive, clutching the poet's poems conspicuously. Professors prowl the aisles. We, the news-room crowd, flatten ourselves against the wall. The hubble-bubble rises around us.

"That's So-and-so. I met him at the Midland Authors' last feed."

"Isn't he dear? I wonder who that . . . "

"What do you s'pose he'll read tonight?"

"Did you see my villanelle in the Scat-book?"

"Isn't it fearfully hawt by this fire?"

"I wonder if it would be a scandal if I smoked a teeny cigarette."

There is a hush near the door; a craning of necks; a flurry of snow as the door opens. There is blown in—The Poet.

He is muffled to the eyes and he is wearing, tonight, his black rain-proof cap, which is so ugly that he idolizes it. He steps forward and beams.

A half dozen people rise from their seats and stretch out hands in vain. The Poet is unbuttoning the tall collar of his ulster. He is as pleased as Punch over the warmth of affection that sweeps toward him; but he does not act like a man receiving homage. He is just the same as when he strolls into the cigar-store and says "Hello, fellows." There is no bunk about The Poet. We see now that he is the same old kid. This is wholesome; we were beginning to be affected by the mawkish worship of the neo-Bohemians and poetasters. He sees us now, and we call to him carelessly, "Hello; how are yu?"

Now he picks his way to his table in front of the fireplace, where priestesses have set up a sort of altar for him, lit with candles, very pretty. But it won't do. Put out the candles, please, and will somebody open a window?

Well, now it seems everything is ready.

[V]

THE POET stands against a background of ochre flames, statuettes, and bon-bon boxes, before the dinky table upon which are piled his books, with shreds of newspaper marking the selected poems. He faces the semi-circle of listeners, swinging his head about so that his gaze takes in everybody. He is in no hurry to begin. Quizzical thoughts seem to stir his lips; his ashen-grey eyes, with their bold, black pupils, twinkle a little with the recognition of people, or perhaps with some inward whimsy. His cragged chin lifts in a curious gesture that throws back his whole head; that head, clothed in its cloak of shining silvered hair, black at the roots, which is—well, the word is "leonine." But what an amiable lion it is! A lion well-fed and purring, it seems; but no moving-picture lion, this; no exhibition lion; sodden with leisure. This is a capricious spirit, capable of stern flashes from under his shaggy grey brows, and of great abstract rages. As the eyelids droop over his deep eyes, and as his lips work, it is anybody's guess what he will say, or read. Will his words scorch the flower-baskets off the green walls? Will they rock the statuettes upon their pedestals?

There is silence now. The more distinguished auditors sit with folded arms, breathless. We of the news-room, nobodies — merely the poet's friends—shuffle our feet where we stand.

The Poet reads.

It is a voice familiar enough, yet charged with a new element. It is a deep voice, deliberate, casual, rich with earth-tones. It comes as though some organist were idly exploring the pedals. What is the voice saying? Mysteries. And gradually there grows upon us news-room visitors a sense of a spell, of being quaintly lost. The figure before us, with its luxurious bangs of grey hair, with the military shoulders and the careless drab clothes, is familiar. Yet it is now remote, inexplicable. Well, there is something we have overlooked. We have seen him write, but we never have heard him read. We have thumbed over his poems, and asked him questions about them, and he has shown them to us and we have given him encouraging grins, but . . . . . boys, we never fathomed him at all. We are fascinated, every one of us, by this public Poet whom we did not know. Nobody in the room is staring at him harder than we. He is changing before our eyes. The companionable chuckle with which he greets us is gone. He has a stern, white look that abashes us. Concentration is cutting that familiar face into hollows. The black pupils blot out the grey of his eyes; deep, deep thought and the memory of creative hours veil the black. And the voice, striking chords that do not dwell in "Good morning" and "Good night," the voice is uttering phrases that we once saw written, that we once ticketed as "good stuff"—and let them go.

Comrades, we never fathomed him. There is something else here, and we can't quite describe it. Those phrases—whence did they come, and whither bound? They are irradiated and clarified by his voice. By his voice those queer masses of printing are explained. The cubes of type melt together, the eruptions of strange, "unpoetic" words acquire a melody. And those maimed sentences that he never chose to finish, those implicatory phrases, like great thumb-marks—complete, complete. His voice is trying to tell us—us, his news-room comrades—what he felt months ago, when all this was written. Up there to his eyrie above the skyscrapers, and out into his starlit nights in the corn-fields, and abroad on his long treks across the deserts—that is where he is trying to take us. But we can follow only a little way; we, whose desks are next to his.

He reads; pauses; reads again. He dips into this book and that. Now we are in the city, tortured and deafened by it. Now we are skimming toward the "sun-burnt west," among purple rocks and powdered trails and the bones of travlers. Now we are on slopes of woodland; and now the baby moon sails and sails in the Indian west, for us. And now we are once more in the city, where broken, work-torn figures are brought to our feet to speak in their horrible, hopeless jargon that we may pity them. The voice of The Poet searches, searches among the meshes of the poems. It comes slow, deep and tender; it comes furious, menacing, sardonic. We are altogether swept away from the city's rigmarole, from our normal moods, from all consciousness of the chic little restaurant. We are sharing The Poet's long-seeing fearless vision; we are learning what his world is.

Very distant at last, the news-room, its clamors and clankings, the babel of nervous voices, the flutter of printed sheets. But from this distance, where The Poet dwells, we regard the news-room in a new light. We share The Poet's grand disdain for successes, and his pity for failures. We see ourselves as part of an immense and tragic procession, in which, despite its shabby ranks and its numerous stragglers, we are proud to march.

And when The Poet has finished, we walk home in the peaceful night, convinced of the majesty of ourselves.

[VI]

TOMORROW morning, if you see us glumly clipping, writing and correcting, and if we seem unchanged, you must still believe us to be under The Poet's spell.

And if you meet The Poet himself on the street, with his gaze fixed on the roof-tops and his very footsteps proclaiming his indifference to time and space, will you please bring him back to the office? The Old Man wants him.

Besides, he belongs here.

{IX}

The Ghost

[1]

IT is mid-summer, and the door of the cigar store stands open, so that we on the benches have a close view of passers-by. They cross the path of our vision, exist for a moment, and vanish. It is the world; it is humanity brought near to us and seeming, when thus foreshortened, ill worth the beholding.

This time it is the news editor, the Star, Campbell and I who muse, gossip, and smoke. Campbell is a man whom I ought to have introduced before. He is a person of some authority and of great lore in recondite questions like the allotment of editorial space and the timing of editions. Privately, he is a philosopher; he goes home to live among tall ghosts of thought, which solace him for the brutal facts to which his working life is devoted. The Star loves to awaken this private passion and see it live, quaintly, amid the architecture of the working day.

So the Star and Campbell, here in the cigar store, are carrying on a metaphysical conversation, far over the heads of the news editor and myself. I hear phrases like "Nietsche! An inverted Baptist"; "No doubt Kant was the underlying cause of the French revolution," and "The theory that man is a time-binding animal . . . ."

Suddenly the news editor leans forward, watches the passing swarm intently, and exclaims:

"Old Slater!"

Campbell looks, and nods.

For my part, I have seen only a disappearing bit of bent shoulder, and a wisp of grey hair. They are gone.

[II]

"LUCKY he didn't look in and see me," says the news editor. "By golly, I dread the sight of the man. Don't know exactly why, either, for it's not a question of his asking me for a job. He's long past that, and he knows it. . . . . Maybe I hate the thought of a 'touch,' though, Lord knows, he's about past that, too. I fancy he'll never show his poor old phiz in our office again. Instead of that,—well, it's a curious thing, but he's present, just the same. He haunts us."

"In what way?" I inquire with a yawn.

"Oh, it's no ghost story; not exactly. It isn't

that his shade inhabits dark corners on late watches. This is a plain, businesslike Chamber of Commerce sort of haunting, that consists of recommendations. You don't think a fellow can haunt an office by means of recommendations; or, rather, by requests for recommendations? Try my job once. Notice the letters I get from snappy employment managers of stores, packing houses, railroads, and so on. Neat letters, with your name sticking through those tissue-covered holes in the envelopes, and a stamped return envelope. All very businesslike. The form generally reads: 'You will oblige us by confidential information about Blank Blank, who says he was employed by you in the years so-and-so; please advise promptly about his character, habits, application to duty; are you relative of applicant, would you re-employ,' and all that tosh. It's through these that old Slater haunts us, fellows. And I always write cheerfully in the forms that he was an A-1 newspaper-man, and is a guy perfectly sober and industrious. I guess I do this so as to lay the ghost; the ghost of his long, sad, grey face."

Campbell takes out his cigar and says: "You can truthfully say that he was a first-class newspaper man. He was that, and more."

"Then how did he blow up?" I inquire.

The news editor and Campbell start to reply simultaneously, and beg pardon.

"You tell it, then."

"No; you know it better. You were here."

So the narrative falls to the metaphysician, who exchanges for this occasion his delight in his illusory world for a certain twinkling zest in the drama of our groundling existence. Meanwhile we gaze vacantly upon the passing figures: Old men, young men, brisk persons, crippled persons, bob-haired women, shawl-covered women, beggars, toilers, blackguards. The personality and the story of Old Slater blend well with this unlovely parade.

[III]

"I'M no great lover of yarns about old days," says Campbell. "Telling them is a habit among newspaper men when they get to a certain age; and after a fellow has listened to all the grey-backed memoirs I have, he may be pardoned if he hesitates to add to them. This business of old Slater has a special tang, though, for me. Probably because I sort of respected the chap. He was very well educated; one might almost call him cultured. We used to have some searching talks when time hung heavy during late watches and so on. He was a great talker, swaggered when he walked, and his opinions were fearfully positive. No doubt he had an inferiority complex."

This exordium Campbell delivers in the meditative way peculiar to him. With a bit more spirit he continues:

"A great, big, broad-stomached, hearty and sports-loving individual was Slater when I first knew him. He could have encircled my neck with one hand. When he sat at the copy desk he didn't slouch, like so many of them, but sat almost bolt upright, making marks on the copy with a flourish almost of disdain. He was very fast, and tireless. It seemed in those days as though we couldn't give him enough to do. While other copy-readers were sweating blood, and groaning between their teeth, Slater would polish off twice as much copy as they, and have plenty of time to sit with his thumbs in his huge waistcoat, gazing around and chuckling.

"Now, a man like that should have been an executive, you may think. But I don't know . . . The Old Man's intuition was very acute. Of course, it may have been that all the responsible jobs were filled. Anyhow, up to the time of the turning point, Slater, with all his education, his skill and his enormous professional blah, remained just a drudge on the desk. He towered among the youngsters, the derelicts, and the riff-raff that we had at that time; he saw a succession of copy-readers tackle the desk, and flunk, either because they were worthless or because they fell foul of our wonderful system. They looked up to Slater in a way. He was the expert; they the bunglers and the never-do-rights. They respected his opinion, too; his opinions so freely uttered on all questions of the day. They fed his vanity. They grumbled in his hearing that he was a powerful sight more competent than the city editor (Franklin, I think it was) and they said he would be a four times better man at the stone than I was. (I was doing make-up at the time.)

"All this naturally swelled old Slater to a ponderable figure in the office. He loomed there at the desk, with his huge head and his balloon-like shirt sleeves, like a relic of some age of mammoth newspaper men. He lent the place dignity. There were legends that he had held a big job under Dana; also that he had edited a paper in Nevada in the mine-rush days. Well, I knew as much about his history as anybody, and the truth was that he had never done anything more sensational than read copy. Just the same, it was impossible to deprive him of his halo. Whenever visiting newspaper men, or former comrades visiting 'the old shop,' came in, they always paused to chat with Slater. And half the time outsiders who called to make requests, or to register kicks with the city editor, mistook the stately Slater for 'the desk.' I remember his austere wave of the hand, and his deep voice: 'Pardon me; see Mr. Franklin.'

"But in spite of all this auto-suggestion that Slater was a great personage, the Old Man never fell for it. There was always a reserve in his manner toward the supposed 'right-hand man of Dana.' He never discussed Slater, for or against;

even exempted him from the periodical razooing that he gave the copy-readers. When he had to call attention to some solecism in Slater's work he would do it quietly, but, I thought, a bit sardonically. There was a curious gravity in his manner toward the big fellow, too, as though he felt he was more of an equal somehow—I don't know. . . . ."

"Devilish cute person, the Old Man; devilish cute," interposes the Star.

"Devilish devilish," puts in the news editor.

"A great judge of men," nods Campbell.

"And of women," grins the Star.

We all grin.

[IV]

"AS I have intimated," continues the narrator, "the Old Man rejected all suggestions that he give Slater a responsible job. If he treated him as an equal it wasn't because he thought him an equal. I suppose it was simply because, with his peculiar sensitiveness to personality, he felt that Slater was of sterner stuff than the majority, and he wasn't quite sure of the result should they —but no use speculating on that. The two swashbucklers continued in an attitude of business-like politeness. The Old Man continued to think that he, and no other, was the greatest newspaper man in the world, and Slater went on feeding his own inferiority complex and hinting that he was a victim of prejudice.

"So we trundled along for some years. And then came the episode that furnishes the point of my foolish old shop yarn.

"I don't suppose this gang recalls much about the Russo-Japanese war, unless some of the ungodly Oriental names we had to learn still stick. We didn't mind the war—although it caused a pernicious lot of late watches—except for the fact that it caught us short-handed. We were more short-handed than ever,—and that was being devilish short. Right on top of it all, and right in the middle of the war, it came time for the telegraph editor's vacation. The Old Man tried to devil him out of it, but the telegraph editor—it was Al Traubel, whom none of you remember—he was a hard-headed son of a gun, and he said to the Old Man: 'Postpone it? No. I've shipped my wife and kids down to the Springs; we've been looking forward to this for a year. I'll pay a "sub"; I'll do anything else you say. But I won't give up this vacation for anybody.'

"Now, the assistant telegraph editor was a drunkard. Couldn't be depended on for an hour. There was nobody handy to shift to the job which, just then, meant a horrible mess of A. P., of special cable, and of emergency problems. And besides—mark this—the censorship in the Far East was veiling and muddling dispatches in a way that passed anything known before or since. A Japanese censor can beat even the British.

"There sat Slater, huge, hearty, competent, voluble, surrounded by prepossessions that he was a whiz of a newspaper man. I recall that the Old Man came in, looked up and down the desk as though searching for someone to wipe his feet on, and then said casually, 'Slater, take the telegraph for a few days, please.' Slater hove his ample body out of one chair into another, seized a wad of copy-paper, and fell to.

"All right. It worked very well. As make-up editor I had a close-up of the fellows on the desk; and nothing could have come to me cleaner, faster, and better-edited than the war stuff as it came from Slater. There had been no decisive event for a while. Matters were working up to the Russian debacle. There were plenty of late watches, however, and these Slater took, working four days a week until midnight, and showing up at seven next morning, fresh as a flower.

"I remember saying to the Old Man: 'We don't seem to miss Al Traubel much, after all.'

"His reply was: 'Never forget how God raised up General Grant.' Which was sarcasm. But when the Old Man is sarcastic, you know, it often means he's pleased.

"The effect of responsibility upon different men is worth watching. Some of them, such as Josslyn, it depresses; others it makes chattery and loose-elbowed. The effect upon Slater was that of expansion. It seemed even to increase his physical bulk. And he let drop more and more remarks that showed how swollen he was getting. He would prate to the youngsters, after the First Final went in, about the pride of the profession; how the profession had its faults, but how we ought to realize what a splendid public service it really was. And mistakes? It wasn't the bawling out, he said, that made bulls serious; it was the departure from professional standards, which was all we had, our whole stock in trade, etc., etc.

"He gave everybody to understand, did old Slater, that if he made a shocking blunder he would just quit; that's all. Not from fear, but from self-disgust.

"And now . . . . . . Well, I'll spare you the fiction flourishes, such as 'a day came,' and all that. What I recall about the episode is that we were sending away the First Final in the usual cyclone of bad temper and balled-up stories (most of my memories are of making up the First Final). We were jamming the type together any old way, and butchering local news until Franklin darned near cried, and trying to watch our proofs during the hullabaloo.

"I remember the Russian story was made up one column wide on the first page, with a head over it something like 'Russians Threaten Revolt.' And just as we were closing, the tail of my eye caught a proof, under a small head following the big one, with the words in it: 'The historic event in the Sea of Japan.' That odd phrase struck me; it warned me, as it were; it set alive a tiny little prescience of trouble. But this warning died under the avalanche of things I had to do. And we went to press.

"Three other afternoon papers went to press at the same hour. Copies of the three were brought up from downstairs at the same time with our paper. All four were laid on my desk together."

Campbell pauses, chuckles, and slaps his knee.

"Oh, those headlines! Thundering Jabberwock!"

"Come now," scoffs the Star, "you're using a story-teller's trick; suspensory pause, and so on. Cut it out!"

"Those headlines said." continues Campbell, "those rival headlines—not ours—said: 'Terrific Naval Battle in Sea of Japan.' 'Togo Defeats Russ in Great Sea Fight.' 'Epoch-Making Naval Engagement; Japanese Reported Victors.' Our big head said; 'Russians Threaten Revolt.' A thundering scoop on us. Every line of it A. P. stuff, too. Stuff that had come to us as well as to them. Professional pride, good-night. Greatness of old Slater, good-night. Oh, Lord!"

And Campbell rocks himself with the memory.

"The Old Man burst into the room with an armful of papers. 'Look at this, and this, and this,' he said to Slater. 'And look what we have —a wretched follow head. You can hardly find our story in the paper. My good Lord, what will people say? How in the devil can I ever explain it?"

"Slater sat upright and bland before the terrible exhibits. He took out a pair of eye-glasses he used on rare occasions, and amiably examined the evidence.

" 'Isn't that curious?' he said (and everybody was listening, you bet.) 'Isn't that curious? Now I never interpreted the dispatch in that way.'

"The Old Man stood back of him, trembling.

" 'Today's historic event in the Sea of Japan' could mean but one thing, Mr. Slater,' he said. 'Haven't we been expecting this battle for days? And as the cable comes from the Japanese, would they release it if it hadn't meant their victory?'

" 'Very good deduction,' smiled Slater. 'But the first rule of the profession is, never make deductions.'

"The Old Man's hair stood on end. He smoothed it down carefully, glared at Slater's fat back, and strode out."

[V]

CAMPBELL takes off his spectacles and wipes them. We see his "philosophical look" coming on.

"About at that period," he says, "must have been when the subconscious in Slater became the conscious. He stepped over the subliminal threshold, and . . . ."

"Come now," I object. "Did he quit, like the good soldier he claimed to be?"

Campbell resumes his spectacles and rubs his nose.

"No. I don't think he did. In fact, I know he didn't. The Old Man was too short-handed to fire him. No; Slater continued on the desk. It would have been hard for some men to come to work at all after a boner like that. But Slater faced it out. He became more expansive and resonant than ever. The rest of us, out of decency, kept quiet about that dispatch; but Slater wouldn't let it rest. He was still talking about it when Roosevelt called the peace conference. He had half a dozen ways of accounting for it, and tried them all out on his silent desk-mates. 'It's funny, you know,' he would say, 'I don't believe I saw that sheet of copy at all; it must have gone out unedited.' Next day it would be: 'Nothing unusual about that little oversight of mine; I remember back on the old Sun . . . .'

"Of course, everybody got sick and tired of the thing. As for the Old Man, I never heard him refer to it after the first day. He kept Slater on telegraph until Traubel got back; but he never addressed him. Just sent in boys with notes, when he had any instructions.

"Well, the incident and the war itself rolled back into history, and Slater, settled down into his old groove, hardly seemed to change at all.

But I can see now that, little by little, he was decaying. His discourses upon topics of the day became more and more vacuous. There came into his eyes a spark of anxiety—not over the quality of his work, but due to the fear, I guess, that people would quit listening to him. He gradually gave up trying to impress the older men and picked out newcomers, cubs, anything, for his audience, switching from foreign affairs to sports, in which he was well versed. After a while he was taken off the local desk, and set to reading sporting copy. Slide number one. Then he moved to the afternoon watch, where he had little to handle except 'specials.' Slide number two. He took to avoiding the staff, and he was found frequently looking into space, with a kind of sadness. He was growing grey-headed.

"The reporters who had played poker with him many a night began to organize their games without him. There were a few of the staff, of course, who secretly rejoiced over his fall, owing to old trifling arguments over their 'stuff.' But on the whole nobody bore him malice. It was simply that as his atmosphere of great man wore out, and his essential puniness showed itself, he dwindled, and dwindled, and shrank into himself. People stopped speaking to him in the elevator; he didn't appear to expect a salutation.

"Only Josslyn, who had become city editor; Josslyn, who overlooks nobody and pities every-

"It may be inferior as fiction," Campbell defends himself. "But I assure you it's psychologically sound."

"Clack-clack" go the feet of the dusty, wrinkled pedestrians, past our door. The voice of the street comes with a note of despair. We consult our watches.

And now, to our confounding, a long, loose phantom of a man, with grey hair crowned by an absurd polo cap, halts at the threshold. He surveys us with a nervous smirk, and enters, holding out a mottled hand to the news editor.

"That little debt," he murmurs, and departs.

The news editor discovers in his hand a mouldy dollar bill.

{X}

The Socialized Copy-Boy

[I]

SOME fifty times a day—oh, nearer a hundred times—the cry goes up from us: "Boy," or "Hey, boy!" Toward edition times that shout, or bark, is heard all over the news-room. It comes from us automatically. "Boy!" What boy? Why, any boy. What are you talking about? Any one of those starvelings on the bench. They're all alike, aren't they? Who knows their names? Who cares who they are, or what they think, or what they wear, so they have legs?

It happens frequently that one of them is fired. The head boy then identifies the departing employe as "You know, the long-nosed boy," or "the boy that wears the brown sweater." This is enough. It is understood that the long-nosed boy is no longer with us, and for that hour, as he retires crestfallen, he is an actuality. But the benchful that is left remains a mere blur of heads and faces, half-visualized, nameless except as a job-lot of consonants.

[II]

HOWEVER, there is Joe; or rather, there was Joe. For he is gone. We got so far as to recognize him as Joe James, which, by the way, was not the name used on the pay-roll. He was on the pay-roll as Valdimir Sziewiscwicz.

He was the boy we hired after he had been fattened at the North Shore camp. A charity lady interceded for him with the city editor, and he "went on" at six dollars a week, which was two dollars less than the scale. We felt that we were rather benevolent as it was.

The charity lady gave us Joe's history in a manner that appealed even to the most "hard-boiled" among us. She pictured Joe's home, which she had seen: The second house west of the C. & N. W. tracks on Iron street; the house with two boards missing from the front steps, and a clothes line in the rear always full of Lilliputian underwear. She pictured Joe's mother, a distracted shrew with a moustache, always stumbling over her own babies; and she described how Joe's mother had thrust Joe down those dangerous steps, yelling: "You got no job you don't come back."

The problem thus presented to Joe was quite insoluble, not only because of his unlovely appearance, but also because of a law; a law which provided that no boy weighing less than eighty pounds could obtain the necessary working certificate, the passport of boydom to the great world of toil. The best Joe could muster was sixty-eight pounds.

The charity lady found him in the ante-room of the school examiner's office, weeping over those missing pounds. He was clearly a case for the Camp, whither he was with some diffiiculty removed. They put him to bed twice a day, and made him lie still under the rough blankets; they fed him milk, gallons of milk; and they taught him how to play, really to play. Every evening they marked on a chart the ascending curve of Joe's weight.

The only time it deflected was the day his mother appeared at the camp, with a kid on each arm, and demanded him, and there was a scene—but let us pass on. In about six weeks Joe tipped the scale at eighty, and despite adenoids and a few other things he passed the school examination and was awarded his work certificate.

It was then that the charity lady called on us.

"And I thought," she said, "that you kind newspaper men would like to help out by giving Joe a position. I do so want him to become a member of society." She beamed upon the city editor and the desk men. "Besides, it would be so nice if you could make a little story of it—what we did for him and all. You could even print photos of him before and—er—after. I could give you some good photos . . . ."

We drew the line at the pictures; but we did "write up" Joe for a merry little half column.

Thereupon, quite unmoved by his distinction, Joe took his place upon the bench among the half-visualized, and we forgot him for a while.

[III]

BUT not for long.
Perhaps a month passed. The news-room floundered on, with its usual dramas, controversies, and excitements. The bench pursued its quarrelsome way, with the average amount of bickerings, of hirings and firings. We still yelled "Hey, boy!" at the bench indiscriminately, nor marked which urchin sprang to the call. Joe, with his close-cropped head, large, stupid eyes and skimpy body, had become absorbed in the melee.

Then the head boy came to the city editor.

"You know that, now, kid got his weight by that camp. He says you should pay him off, as he got to quit."

"What! scowled the city editor. "What boy?"

Patient explanation.

"Oh, that one. Well, what's wrong with him?"

The head boy shifted from one foot to the other.

"Well, he says account he lives at home now

he's lost two pounds, and so he can't work no more."

The city editor called his assistant.

"See about it, will you?" he begged; and plunged his nose into a pile of copy.

The assistant investigated. He even consulted authorities, learning thereby that to maintain Joe at par would require some two pints of milk per diem. It seemed unnecessary to tell the city editor about this. The obvious thing was to supply the milk; and, in order that the expense might not fall upon the office treasury, thus upsetting various sacred rules, the assistant city editor took up a collection among the Star, the Drunkard, Josslyn and a few others of "the crowd," and a restaurant downstairs supplied Joe's milk at cost. The school authorities, consulted by telephone, grandly permitted the Great Example to continue at work provided only that he be weighed each week by them, and be maintained at normal.

Faithfully did the Joe's Milk Society hew to the line. Once a week the head boy took up the collection; twice a day he escorted Joe to the restaurant and prevailed upon him to swallow the milk. The matter fell into the routine; it became automatic, like keeping the assignment book or sweeping out the office. Thus are the little variations of our news-room life drifted over by the sands of the commonplace.

The next thing that came up was a question of

working-hours. In this we enjoyed the enthusiastic interference of our old friends the school authorities. I don't know how many records they had Joe card-indexed in; but now they dug up one that stumped us. Solemnly each week they had weighed him and passed him; with suspicion, I suppose, they had marked the fact that he continued to draw six dollars a week. And now, with an efficiency suitable to the enforcement of a law occupying several pages in the statute-book, they brought forward the fact that Joe required more schooling.

"Form AAZ," the notice read. "You are hereby informed that your employe Vladimir Sziewiscwicz must attend continuation school four (4) hours a week——."

The city editor slammed the notice on the floor.

"What's all this about? Good Lord, the things a fellow gets in the mail. I say, Frank, see about it, will you?"

The suave assistant picked up the crumpled notice, and by some inquiry discovered that Vladimir S—etc., meant Joe. There was a session of the milk guarantors, and the suggestion was put forward that if Joe was to become a member of society some way must be found of keeping him at work and at the same time sending him to school. The head boy brought up the point that in this event he must add another member to the bench. The addition was at once authorized by the assistant city editor, and the following red-tape started unwinding: (1) examination and approval of the new boy's work certificate; (2) order to cashier placing him on pay-roll; (3) entry of new name on pay-roll; (4) issuance of identification check, locker key, etc.; (5) drawing up of new pay-check; (6) checking against pay-roll to make sure amount correct; (7) auditing of revised aggregate pay-roll by auditor; (8) recording of revised figures on three or four index cards; (9) identification of new boy as the one entitled to check; (10) cashing of check at pay-clerk's window. I mention these things only to suggest the social forces put into play by establishing a member of society.

Yes, the advent of Joe began to be felt in other departments than ours. It was presently felt in the medical department, which consisted of two doctors in an office around the corner. They had not had a case from our shop for over a year, and the placard on the wall saying "In case of accident, notify Dr. B——" had become illegible from dust. But Joe became a case. He reported one morning with an angry-looking patch of skin on his right forearm, more or less covered by court-plaster. It developed that he had scratched himself the day before on the pneumatic tube leading to the composing room. He exhibited the wound to the head boy, who thought nothing of it. Nobody thought anything of it. The bench was always getting itself bruised, or black-eyed, or consumptive. But after a few days Josslyn, passing on his way to lunch, noticed Joe's arm. It was swollen to astounding dimensions and bound with loathsome rags. The sight stopped the compassionate Josslyn in his tracks.

"What on earth's happened to you?" he demanded.

Joe merely rolled his large, stupid eyes.

"Sore arm," he mumbled.

"But have you had a doctor?"

Joe looked blank.

Then Josslyn hailed the city editor. Had he seen this kid's arm? Ought the kid be allowed to work?

"Gad, I haven't time to inspect their arms," complained the C. E. Nevertheless, he took time to inspect Joe's; and a copy-reader or two strolled over, and somebody remarked "blood poison." Joe met the inspection and remarks dispassionately. But once, when someone inquired, "Does it hurt?" his eyes filled with tears, and for a moment he seemed human.

The fact emerging that he had been scratched upon our pneumatic tube, and not any pneumatic tube belonging to the S——, etc., family, it seemed proper to invoke the privilege of calling up Dr. B——. The doctor entered into the matter with alacrity. Not so Joe, however. He grumbled, he protested, he showed every sign of fear, at last he fought—like many other beings in process of being made members of society. But, being practically one-armed, he could not prevail against the head boy and the numerous volunteers from the bench.

A small procession, consisting of Joe, the head boy and Josslyn, followed the little-known path to the doctor's office, pausing on the way for milk. They returned with the arm in a beautiful bandage and a wondering look in Joe's eyes.

I realize that these incidents do not carry an ascending curve of interest. Joe did not die. His arm "went down," both as a swelling and as an event. But, to prove that establishing him in the status in which we were establishing him carries consequences of some sort, consider these results: (1) Three signatures to be obtained to a document resembling an income tax schedule, describing the accident, the parentage of Joe, and so on; (2) a physician's bill very simply conceived, but requiring the signature of four department heads before being valid; (3) an order permitting Joe to remain at home with full pay; (4) a written explanation to the ever-vigilant school people that he was absent from school owing to circumstances beyond our control; (5) the sudden awareness of the Old Man—through his having to sign two of the documents—that Joe existed as an office problem.

[IV]

THE Old Man, however, did not yet know Joe by sight. Perhaps, indeed, he never came to do so. I don't know that even the catastrophe next following shocked the Old Man as it did us.

For some weeks after the medical incident nothing happened to our Great Example. Glancing casually at him, we seemed to observe that he was looking more prosperous, as well as rather more than half-witted. The milk contributions had stopped. Joe had safely and permanently passed the eighty mark. The school people had stopped weighing him. He came down every morning, went blindly but faithfully about his tasks, and had nothing to say.

But one afternoon, when there was hell of some sort popping—I believe it was a Board of Trade failure—the unlucky destiny of the Sziewiscwicz line showed itself once more.

The Old Man, who was considerably excited by the failure, had made several trips into the newsroom, asking questions and giving orders. Most of us knew when he was coming—we knew his step a mile away—and when he approached the swing door from the news room into the hall, his mere shadow was enough to make us stand aside. About two o'clock he started to come through, with his gaze, as usual, fixed some five feet above the floor. Just then Joe started to gallop out the other way, carrying a proof with a rush correction.

He hit the door like a small battering ram, flung it smartly against the Old Man's knuckles and knees; and then he tried to squeeze past the managing editor's large bulk and escape.

The boss, with half the breath knocked out of him, snatched at Joe's shoulder, but missed. Joe sprawled on all fours; but his instinct of escape from authority gave him new strength, and he made off down the hall, dropping the corrected proof as he fled.

As soon as the Old Man could recover he stuck his head in at the door, and yelled to all the executives in sight: "Fire that boy! Fire him at once."

Rueful glances went about the desk.

The Old Man (dusting his knees)—"What boy was that?"

City Editor—"I didn't notice. Did anybody see which boy it was?"

Silence.

Old Man (to head boy)—"You know who it was. Speak up."

Head Boy—"It's a lad we call Joe."

Old Man—"Well, bounce him." (To city editor): "Damn it, Brown, what do you have those calf-headed Bohunks around here for? I'll make an example of him."

City Editor (with a sly look at Josslyn)— "We've been figuring he was an example already. You see, sir, he's the kid we got from the camp where he was fattened. He's an unusual case. He . . . ."

Old Man—"Fat or lean, out he goes. Now see here, I don't think these figures on the liabilities . . . ."

And that was all of that. Reluctantly we gave Joe his hat, and an order for his pay, and broke it to him that he was severed from the pay roll. He took the news easily, and clumped out of the office without regrets or good-byes. Well, so long, Joe.

I was not present the next day when a Slavic gentleman with a very radical moustache, bulging eyes and dirty overalls, came up to see the city editor, dragging a small urchin called Vladimir, but I heard about it. It seems the low-browed person offered to break every bone in the boy's body if we so desired. The low-browed person offered apologies to our honorable newspaper for the conduct of his son; he took off his cap to the assistant city editor, who went out to see him; and renewed the bone-breaking offer. The A. C. E., alarmed, advised against this solution. "You see, Joe didn't do anything much," he told the elder Bohunk. "It wasn't serious at all." Whereupon the bone-breaker bade a polite adieu to the A. C. E. and dragged Joe away with him.

So ended that lesson.

[V]

CHRISTMAS began to approach. I mention Christmas not in order to lend a new and saccharine element to this tale, but because with Christmas came always a new set of problems surrounding the bench, a new spirit entirely among the mob of boys. The office had a custom of giving a turkey to each employe. It was noticeable that discipline on the bench improved as Christmas came near. Sometimes, too, there seemed to be an unusually large membership.

The quota this December was considerable. The city editor had called the head boy to him and had declared: "Don't you hire any more of 'em now, do you hear me?"

About December 20 a very familiar figure was found one morning sitting on the bench. The only unfamiliar thing about it was that it wore long trousers. Barring this, it bore a striking resemblance to a member colloquially known as Joe, but officially as Sziewiscwicz.

How did this materialization accord with the orders given to the head boy? That was the question asked in whispers on the copy desk. Had Josslyn interceded for Joe? No, Josslyn had not. The attention of the other members of the defunct milk society was called to the apparition. "Oh, I suppose Frank (the assistant city editor) got him put back. It's nearly Christmas, you know.

But Frank denied having done this. In fact, he looked alarmed and went over to the head boy, and without meeting Joe's appealing eyes, inquired: "What's this kid doing here?"

"He's just visiting," explained the head boy.

"Oh! Visiting!"

The copy desk suppressed smiles.

Here the city editor, annoyed by the voices, looked up. He, too, became aware of the presence of Joe. He got up and went over to the bench, and spoke with undue gentleness.

"I don't think it looks very well for you to visit here, Joe," he said. "You'd better go."

The head boy looked embarrassed.

"Can I speak to you at your desk a minute, Mr. Brown?" he begged. Permission given, he followed his chief to the desk, where he bent over him and mumbled earnestly for quite a while.

As we learned later, the plea involved the following details: Joe had saved out of his earnings, both what we paid him and what he had gained by odd jobs later, enough to purchase on part payments the long-trousered suit he now wore. It was the only suit he had, those of previous winters having descended to his small brothers. "Well, his father, now," the head boy may be imagined saying, "his father says he won't let him go out of the house Christmas; he'll take his clothes away and make him stay in bed, account he's got only one suit you see that's what he'll have to do, unless . . . ." And the alternative made Brown first swear and then laugh. The alternative was that Joe must get back his job on the paper. Yes, that was it, incredible as it sounds; Joe must be hired back or stay in bed all day Christmas.

I heard the city editor and his assistant discussing it.

"Of course, I can't let that bulldozing Bohunk put it over," he said. "Fine chance."

"It ain't the kid's fault," mused the assistant.

The city editor tapped his desk with his pencil for some minutes.

"He was a good kid, wasn't he?" he seemed to remind himself. "But," he broke out, on a sudden thought, "he's the one who crashed into the Old Man at the door. Gee, I'd forgotten that."

"The Old Man would never remember him," murmured the assistant. "He's got long trousers now."

There was a pause, and the city editor's face lit up.

"Say, I'll put him on as an extra till after Christmas," he announced. "Then we'll can him again, see?" And he sent for the head boy.

I heard this conversation, and I record it because it is typical of the things that make us fond of Brown, and that make us fond of our crowd as a whole, and of the news-room atmosphere generally. Oh, yes, we break all the rules of 100 per cent efficiency and economy sometimes; and we contradict ourselves; and we act like fools trying to make people members of society; and altogether we're a shiftless, a cynical and untruthful crew. And we put Joe back on the pay-roll under an entirely new name; and we taught him to keep his head down when he passed the Old Man (though the Old Man never looked at him twice). And Joe walked home with the biggest turkey of the lot that Christmas, besides getting his share of the $5.75 the staff contributed as the annual Yuletide donation to the bench. To cap the climax, Brown forgot to take Joe off from the pay-roll after Christmas was over, and he stayed at work, drawing six dollars a week and picking up a dime now and then for extra errands.

The years pass. Joe's limbs grow thick and powerful. He begins to have a slight moustache. He is reliable, and "runs" even the Old Man's proofs with distinction. He is spoken of for head boy. He is a success. The experiment——

[VI]

ONE day not long ago the city editor met the charity lady at a committee meeting.

"Oh, Mr. Brown," she gushed. "I'd so like to know what became of that boy—really, I don't recall his name—the one you so kindly gave a position to after his treatment at the camp. Is he still in your office?"

"No," replied Brown. "He isn't."

"Dear, dear; I'm sorry. I thought it would be such a nice position for him."

"It was," said Brown. "Yes, it was a good place for Joe. We did everything for him we could; and I suppose that as a sociological experiment it was A number 1. But . . . ."

"Do tell me about it."

"Well, you see, he was raised two dollars a week. We thought that was pretty good—considering everything. But about two months after he got the raise, he—well, I remember that just as I was cleaning up copy for the Home Edition one day the shadow of a stocky form fell across my desk, and although I was trying to talk to three other people at once this person insisted on talking to me. It was our friend Joe, now nearly full grown (for a Bohunk), well fed, confident, sophisticated, argumentative, and angry. He looked at me with smoldering black eyes from under a safe-blower's cap he was wearing. And he said, 'Mr. Brown, I got to have more money, see, or I quit, see?' I was very busy, so I said—well, it was to the effect that he should retire at once. He swaggered out of the office, and that was the last we saw of him."

"I'm sorry," bewailed the charity lady. "I never dreamed he would become that sort of person, after so much kindness."

"Well," said Brown (and I don't suppose he meant it cynically at all), "at least we admit that Joe became quite a typical member of society."

{XI}

The Triumphant Comma-Hound

[I]

SOMETIMES, although rarely, Josslyn tells us a story. He is full of fables of the news room, this "old inhabitant." We like to sit about, with our feet cushioned upon piles of early editions, and listen to his narratives. And we like, too, to watch the changes upon Josslyn's serene face, and the growing warmth that brings back his youth. Yes, and we laugh more heartily, perhaps, than his humor demands.

This afternoon he told us the story of the Triumphant Comma Hound. I give it, not quite in his words, and excluding most of the technicalities. I forget what evoked the story; perhaps that egregious but no longer shocking typographical error of three editions since, when a bank was referred to by the clearing house as "solvent," and the paper declared it "insolvent."

But to the story; or rather, the paraphrase.

[II]

IT was one soggy, dark, dreadful morning some ten years ago. The "gang" had got in late that morning. Everybody's brain was like mush. It was the same in the composing room as in the news-room; the disgusting soot blanket of the city seemed to have closed down over one's head. The printers worked droopily. Editors collided with them. There were peevish exchanges. The first edition was sent away ten minutes late.

During the lull before the next edition, Josslyn says, the feeling got about the news-room that something was sure to go wrong; or already had. Sometimes you aren't certain what may lurk for you among the ample folds of the paper just issued. "I remember," said our raconteur, "that Frank Wade, the head copy-reader (this was just before I quit the city desk), called over to me that morning: "I'm using all four eyes today. It seems to drip errors."

Still, Josslyn shaped up his work for the next edition, the "Market Special," without much thought of trouble. He went to lunch, as usual, just after his copy was all out; and returned in his wonted twenty minutes in time to meet the printed papers coming up the elevator under a boy's arm. Josslyn stepped inside the door of the news-room, letting the boy squeeze by him. Before he had time to seize a paper the boy had dumped the bundle on the copy desk, and the terrible discovery was made by Wade.

"Great gosh, fellows, look at this!" was the "head's" horrified yell. Josslyn gave one look, and—well it was awful enough!

The copy-readers seized their papers with a single motion, and spread them out. Murmurs of "Holy sailors!" and "Well, of all the dymnation——"

They were looking, with varying attitudes of awe, stupefaction or amusement, at the big two-column head at the right hand of the page. This headline (in at least 36-point) read:

"BLODGETT IS THIEF."

The subordinate line—"pyramid," Josslyn called it—followed, with astounding inconsequence, or subtle logic, as one chose to look at it:

"Well-Known Banker Elected President
of Chamber of Commerce."

The Drunkard (just then in favor) caught hold of a chair in mock panic, and shouted: "Some paper today, fellows! Come and look at it."

Everybody was looking at it. Josslyn confesses he was too stunned for a moment to act. Frank Wade recovered himself first, rushed to the 'phone, and started howling for the pressroom to stop the run. There were explosions of laughter and profanity all through the room. A copy-boy seized upon the occasion to fall over backward in his chair with a devastating crash. Josslyn stood fingering the paper, **his** paper of whose reputation he thought so much, with that furious libel on top of one of his stories—the story that was being at that moment fed out to the financial district with the motto in an "ear" on the corner of the page: "Latest and Most Reliable Market Reports."

The Drunkard mounted a chair and read, as though at a public meeting:

"BLODGETT IS THIEF.

"Well-Known Banker Elected President of Chamber of Commerce."

But just then there was a hush; a truce alike upon hilarity and debate. The Old Man came in. He grasped a copy of the paper in both hands.

The copy-readers dropped into their chairs as though at drill. The Drunkard sprang to the floor, and started to whistle. Josslyn advanced to meet the Old Man.

[III]

HE says the calm of the managing editor was admirable. But one can imagine the way his eyes must have glittered through his well-known spectacles, and how like marble his jaw was set.

"Have you stopped the run?" were the Old Man's words.

"I've been 'phoning," cried Wade from the booth, "but I can't get a connection."

"Don't waste your highly valuable energy

then," said the Old Man. "By this time the edition has been printed—fortunately or unfortunately, as may be."

He walked up to the copy-desk, and only then, Josslyn says, could it be seen how his powerful hands were trembling.

"If any gentleman who writes heads," he remarked placidly, "if any journalist here present sent out a head reading that way, I invite him to take my place in the county jail after Mr. Blodgett brings criminal libel proceedings. And I invite him to draw the pay due him at once. In fact . . . ."

A copy-reader whose name Josslyn recalls only as "Ruddy" rose from his seat and spoke like a child at school:

"I wrote that head, Mr. Thain. I—I swear I wrote it 'chief.' "

" 'Chief,' not 'thief' ?" in the Old Man's most punctilious tone.

"Sure, I wrote it 'Blodgett Is Chief,' just like that. Believe me, Mr. Thain . . . ."

But the Old Man had already started for the composing room. Josslyn flitted at his elbow; Frank Wade and a couple of others followed the Old Man's dark, brooding bulk. A "curious throng," as the News Bureau says, trickled after at a distance.

Somebody in the procession murmured a "secret" known to all: "Why, Blodgett is one of

Mr. Jefferson's best friends! A swell thing to hang on the composing room." And somebody else: "I wonder who the poor devil of a proofreader is, and what he'll get."

You see, everybody figured that, whoever he was, the proofreader was bound to be a poor devil. Proofreaders (commonly called "comma-hounds") are that, anyway. Ask the copy-desk.

[IV]

"I WAS considerably dazed as we entered the composing room," Josslyn said. "I hardly knew what was going on. But," giving us one of those glimpses of his reflective nature, "I felt, as I often do, the majesty of the place. Yes, majesty! The composing room, for me, has twice the class of the news-room. The beat of the linotypes alone, the queer rushing sound, like showers of warm rain, gives one a feeling of scope, of—er, I don't know what. And everything, except maybe at the stone, is so orderly, so heavy with tradition. You feel the unity of that gang of workers, their craft-pride; you get a sense of rules upon rules. And you divine how men have become cogs in this mass of machinery, how they turn, turn, until they wear out. Especially the comma-hounds."

We politely endured this digression. Someone remarked, "I don't suppose the Old Man was thinking about that as he bore down on Big Jim."

Josslyn was certain he was not. The Old Man

was out to demolish something. He tramped down the aisle between the linotypes, uttering not a word. The floor shook under him.

Arrived at the stone with his accusing copy of the paper still clasped in both hands, he found Big Jim in the center of a circle of printers, some grinning, others scratching their heads with ink-black fingers. An old fellow with a leather apron and a stained beard was doing a lot of explaining to the foreman. He was the man who set up the head.

"I just picked out o' the wrong box," he was saying. "Might 'a' happened to anybody. I just picked out o' the wrong box . . . ."

The Old Man burst into this leisurely postmortem like Death itself visiting a coroner's inquest.

"Mr. Muldoon," he said, in the high, arrogant way he kept for such encounters, "I suppose you have seen this—this pleasing example of typography. I only wonder your men did not set it in ninety-six point, although ordered in thirty-six."

"I've seen it; yes, Mr. Thain," replied Big Jim. He was a head taller than the Old Man, and a heap more combative.

"Well, what would you suggest doing about it?"

"I would suggest that you leave that to me," answered Jim, folding his great, muscle-ridged arms.

The Old Man swung his gaze about, as though

to overawe the entire membership of the typographical union, if possible—also to see whether the editors present were listening.

"The trouble with this place," he declaimed, "is that there's no penalty—no penalty. Mistakes like this will go on in this composing room indefinitely. No one will be fired."

The printers, safe though they were under the shadow of Big Jim, shrank before the Old Man's spectacles. The foreman, however, only remarked: "What you'd better be doin' is to see if your editor wrote the head so my man could read it."

Approving murmurs from the printers; murmurs of, "You bet! Plenty of blind handwriting nowadays."

"Send for the copy," blurted the Old Man. "Have you got the copy?"

Then he had another thought.

"Who read proof on this? Must have been one of that new crew you hired. They've been letting things go by for weeks."

Big Jim grinned.

"One of the new crew, eh? Look here, Mr. Thain, I'll let you have a look at the proofreader who O. K.'d this head. He's no chicken. It was old Johnny Donahue, and no other. Old Johnny."

This name, which may have meant something to Big Jim, carried no idea at all to the visiting editors, Josslyn said. It was odd, too. They thought they knew everybody in the composing room. Yet Jim's words described someone who had worked for years in the comma-hounds' kennel, and never had shown his face to an editor; never had walked in at a busy time and argued about the meaning of a word like "transpired" or "penetrated"; never had come up to the stone and said, "Look here, I suppose you'll say this is all right, but I can't make sense of it"; never—and this was strangest of all—never had requested free tickets to the poultry show or the six-day bicycle race. Who was this man? Why, Johnny Donahue!

"Send for Donahue," ordered Big Jim. A galley boy went scurrying.

There was a pause in the interchange of courtesies. The audience at the clinic hung about talking in whispers. Our Old Man, upon whose forehead gleamed drops of perspiration, stood and scowled at the words, "Blodgett Is Thief." The great swish of the machines went on in waves. The tall clock grimaced down over the room.

And suddenly it was found, Josslyn dramatically declared, that Mr. Jefferson was among them. How he had arrived so silently no one knew. He had come without warning; he had not been sent for. In fact, this manifestation was without precedent.

Josslyn remembers that the owner wore an elegant black morning-coat, and carried eye-glasses pinned to his silken lapel. His grey moustache was neatly trimmed. He might have been on his way to an audience at the White House.

[V]

THE news of the owner's arrival in person traveled electrically up and down the ranks of machines. Heads appeared here and there, popping up in unexpected places. It was a lull in the morning's work, anyhow; the lull became a recess. By twos and threes printers stole up to the edge of our group, until the assemblage suggested a union chapel meeting. A knot of galley boys jostled and winked at a distance. Everything hung fire, awaiting Mr. Jefferson's words.

That he was very angry nobody needed to be told.

But though angry, and hurt, and perhaps a bit rattled, the owner showed his employes the quality of his self-control. He was more deliberate than the Old Man; he was calmer than Big Jim. Evidently during the few minutes since he had seen that appalling head he had felt, digested, and lived down the emotions that still racked his responsible editors. The only evidence of unusual disturbance was the fact that he had invaded the composing room, instead of sending for somebody. He had to know at once, hear with his own ears, the reason why his friend Blodgett had been set down a 36-point thief.

"Now, just who did this?" he inquired in gentlemanly tones. His level gaze was fixed at a point midway between the Old Man and Jim.

As for those gentlemanly tones, not an editor or printer doubted that they veiled the intention of scalping somebody; or maybe everybody. "After a bull like that, what would you expect?" Josslyn asked us.

Well, just who did this? was what Mr. Jefferson wanted to know. The elderly printer who set up the head was seen to swallow hard. However, while the owner's question still hung unanswered there was a slight commotion at the edge of the crowd, and up strolled the ancient comma-hound, the mysterious Mr. Donahue, who had put a damning "O. K." upon that "Blodgett Is Thief."

"We knew him at once," Josslyn said. "I'm sure none of us had seen him before, but his type was unmistakable. Sparse white hair, tired eyes, narrow, stoop shoulders—all the rest of it. He was a little fellow with a queer hobble, and yet a remnant of dignity. As he came forward, he didn't seem the least bit impressed, or alarmed, or remorseful. He was in his shirt sleeves, and kept his hands in his pockets; didn't even take 'em out when he faced the owner."

It must have been worth seeing, that encounter. Josslyn had by this time almost forgotten the nature of the "bull," he was so interested in the contrast between erect, dapper, fully competent Mr. Jefferson and the poor little spindleshanks with his blinking eyes and his underfed look;

the contrast between authority and humility; the eternal and dreadful contrast between success and failure. If they had searched all the business offices and second-hand stores and old people's homes in town to find somebody to enact the part of Failure in this morality play they couldn't have discovered a better actor than old Johnny Donahue. The only thing was, he wasn't at all aware of it. He seemed only mildly interested in the show. Apparently he wanted to get the interruption in his work over with, and go back to his coop.

When Mr. Jefferson put up his eye-glass and studied the human wisp that had been brought before him, he appeared a little nonplussed. He glanced around at Big Jim, who said: "This is the man, sir, who read the proof of that head. He let the blunder go by; he put his initials on the proof, meaning 'O. K.' Then, you see, in the rush at the stone——"

Mr. Jefferson waggled his head impatiently, and Jim stopped.

"So you are the proofreader," said the owner.

Donahue looked at him stolidly, with his pink-rimmed blue eyes.

"There's eight of us in there altogether," he began. But Big Jim spoke up: "Mr. Jefferson wants to know how you come to let that bull go by. Wake up now, Johnny, and let's have the answer."

Donahue stood there with his hands in his pockets, apparently thinking hard. Evidently the problem interested him. A nice professional problem, really.

"When I was editor of a paper," he at last replied, in his thin quaver, "I used to ask the boys that. I dunno's I ever got the right answer. I dunno's that there is any answer."

"You were editor of a paper?" The owner's tone was inscrutable.

"Yes, sir; the Cherryville Democrat. But o' course that doesn't mean I would be competent to edit—well, this paper, for instance. Mine was only a little paper; and all that was thirty years ago."

"Where have you worked since?"

"Here."

"For thirty years?" The owner put up his eyeglass again. "As proofreader throughout?"

"Yes, sir. Right in that same coop there." Old Johnny winked affectionately at Big Jim.

There was a pause. The spectators had begun to lose their shocked appearance. The Old Man seemed to be breathing more freely. And yet— could Mr. Jefferson let this thing pass without at least "docking" somebody?

He cleared his throat, took out a large monogrammed handkerchief and touched his moustached lips with it.

"Thirty years ago," he said (and he seemed to have quite forgotten the crowd about him), "my father was publisher of this paper."

"I know it," grinned old Johnny. "He hired me."

The owner actually smiled.

"Yes, he used to hire and—er—fire the hands himself. But—ahem—we are getting away from the point of all this. . . . Of course, you understand, Mr. Donahue, that this is a very serious thing to have happen to the Press. We shall be a laughing-stock for days, if no worse. That is aside from the fact that Mr. Blodgett will feel very much injured; an estimable man, Mr. Blodgett. Now do you think, Mr. Donahue, that I can let the matter pass?"

"No, sir," was old Johnny's reply. "I suppose I'm canned."

"I was going to suggest . . . ." began Big Jim, but Mr. Jefferson again held up his hand.

"I am not yet clear," he said to the proofreader, "how you could overlook the error; how you could fail to see that large black T; why you didn't change it."

Donahue scratched his head.

"I been trying to remember ever since I saw the Market Edition. Now, o' course, I did see that T; it's no use sayin' I didn't see it. I ain't blind." He glanced whimsically around the circle of listeners. "I guess I must 'a' thought the editor meant to write it that way. I guess I must 'a' thought 'Maybe this Blodgett is a thief' and I must 'a' thought 'I suppose they're willing to chance a libel suit.' But, good Lord, man, what's the use bothering about what I thought? It's all got pretty dim to me, what editors do things for. I used to go briskin' around asking editors why this and why that, but . . . ."

He paused and eyed Mr. Jefferson, expecting a verdict. Everybody expected it. But Mr. Jefferson only leaned back against a truck, and pondered. Presently Big Jim seemed to wake up. He glared about at the crowd, and shouted: "Back to work, you skulkers. Th' home edition 'll be on us first thing you know."

The eager listeners faded. Linotype men, "make-ups" and galley boys ambled off to their tasks. There remained at length only the owner, the Old Man, the foreman, Josslyn—and the culprit. Amid this diminished assemblage Mr. Jefferson still leaned against the truck, dangling his eye-glasses. Finally he said:

"Donahue, I have a large private library in this building, as you may have heard. It needs cataloguing. Would you like the job?"

The old proofreader blinked, glanced at Big Jim, sidled back and forth a moment on his heels, and shook his head.

Upon this, according to Josslyn, Mr. Jefferson, without uttering another word, strode down the aisle between the machines and out of the composing room, his head lowered in thought. The Old Man, looking disappointed, followed.

And old Johnny hobbled back to his coop.

[VI]

"THAT'S all," said Josslyn, with a benign glance around.

"You don't mean to finish with such an anticlimax as that," complained one of us. "Wasn't the old bird fired?"

"Of course not. He kept at work until he died, three years ago.

I thrust in a surmise of my own: "I suppose the remorse over his blunder pursued him to the grave."

Josslyn laughed.

"Remorse! We all forgot the thing within two days. Of course, we printed a first-page skinback: 'Regrettable typographical error' and so on. But Donahue I'll tell you what happened to him: He became locally famous. He was the man who had stood up to the boss and had got away with it. He became a hero. Everybody forgot what the blunder was, but nobody forgot that something or other had put old Johnny into the limelight. No longer was he a wraith in a cave—a ghost who didn't even haunt anybody—but he became a personage to whom people said 'Good morning, Mr. Donahue. in the elevator. He was pointed out to visiting printers: 'That's Donahue. He don't look much, but he's a friend of the owner's.' The triumphant comma-hound gained flesh, stood up straighter, wore better clothes. I've heard, indeed, that his work became practically perfect."

Josslyn's listeners looked skeptical.

"Now tell us he got a raise on the strength of his bull, and the yarn'll be complete," someone said.

"No, not that," smiled Josslyn. "Not quite like that. But I'll tell you what did happen: About two months after the famous post-mortem, old Johnny wandered into the Old Man's office, teetered on his heels a moment, then stuck out his jaw, and says he: 'Mr. Thain, I've got a little favor to ask; if you could spare 'em, would you kindly let me have a couple of tickets to the poultry show?"

{XII}

Josslyn

PART ONE

[I]

IT has come time to deal adequately with this character, that has hovered on the margin of one portrait after another. It could not help coming in. For although Josslyn never obtrudes himself upon the news-room, he is in fact the most pervasive being whom we have—unless it be the Old Man—the oftenest quoted, the oftenest consulted. And yet there is no one about whom we have known less. To deal adequately with him presents difficulties.

I offer acknowledgments, first of all, to the Star, who has sat in the cigar store with Josslyn for many an hour, and has drawn from him, bit by bit, the torn manuscript of his experience. There is a sympathy between these two. The aging, sweet-natured veteran looks tenderly upon the boy with his outbursts and his foibles; and the whirling brain of the Star seems to come to rest, to rest gladly and admiringly, in the presence of the man who has attempted so much, been disappointed so often, and yet retained goodness.

An elderly printer is another of my authorities for this sketch. He remembers when Josslyn came to the news-room. That was a long time back, alas! The printer recalls a day when, strolling into the editors' zoo to beg some favor, he noticed a "new guy" sitting at a desk; a youth with more legs than body, and more eyes than anything else. The printer, a sociable creature, said to him: "Say hand me that paper over there, will you?" and added, out of suddenly-born instinct: "Thanks." The youth smiled wanly and replied: You are quite welcome." The printer went away mysteriously impressed.

And then, there is a man once a staff photographer, but now grown rich in the "movies," who sometimes relates anecdotes of his leaner past, and who recollects how he and Josslyn went on assignments when both were young. He tells of a fire which they "covered"; a small fire in a hospital. It was out when they arrived, but there were nurses to be photographed and interviewed. Josslyn, says the photographer with a chuckle, was too timid to cross the street and ply the nurses with questions; so the photographer did this for him. And Josslyn wrote out the notes on the train and brought into the office a fairly good story. The photographer, never having met a timid reporter, questioned Josslyn deftly, and found out that he was a Phi Beta Kappa, and had been intended for a professor of English, but that he liked journalism much better—or at least thought he would like it.

"It's a tough game," the photographer warned him. "It eats chaps like you alive."

But Josslyn, he says, only shook his head smilingly. As they all do.

[II]

THE STAR'S discoveries go farther back than this; back to a village settlement which lay near the city, but remained quite isolated from it. Although the smoke clouds, growing bigger year by year, were clearly visible on the horizon, and at night the flares of furnaces furnished a sulky Aurora, the storms and fevers of our turbulent center never reached Happyville, as the village was called. Josslyn's parents were quiet folk, with a fondness for Browning and Wordsworth, a dislike of Emerson, a positive horror of Robert Ingersoll. Their favorite quotations were "God's in His heaven," and "All things work together for good." Their theory of bringing up children was to shield them from all knowledge of evil; even to deny them newspapers that featured crime. Their idea was to create an atmosphere of love that would shut out the world, to breathe into their son and daughter their own pure and gracious natures, and to shape these children into fragile, trustful creatures like themselves. They succeeded.

"But what becomes of children like that after the parents are gone?" asks the Star with his wry smile. Josslyn could answer the question; so, perhaps, could the sister whom he has always cherished. (For, it seems, he has never married.)

What happened to Josslyn was that, immediately after he left college, with an excellent degree and an ability to write masterful critiques of the English poets, both the parents died, and a different face was put upon everything. Goodbye, haloed professorship of English! It was a case of supplying immediate wants. Fanny, the sister, went to work in a library. Arthur, the brother, took his writing talent into the nearest market.

In his narrative to the Star he skipped over most of the period during which he knocked at doors. We find him suddenly entering a newspaper office in search of a "staff position." Not the Press, though, this first one; it was the old Times, whose owner in those days was a very religious man, and had known Professor Josslyn in denominational affairs. Perhaps Mrs. Josslyn suggested that Arthur consult this journalistic friend; we do not know. But Arthur sat for an hour in the luxurious ante-room of Ransom, editor of the Times, and then was received, only to be handed a card on the back of which was written the words: "Mr. Blather, I refer Mr. Josslyn to you."

"Give this to our managing editor," said the kindly Ransom. "So sorry to hear of your eminent father's death."

Blather was kind too. He gave Arthur a minute and a half, asked him one question—"What newspaper experience have you had?"—and regretted that the staff was full.

Arthur went out into the street, both downcast and exhilarated. A mere glance about the editorial rooms, a mere hint of the subdued professional bustle of the place, had cast over him the miserable shroud of his timidity. And yet at the same time, it had given him a strange delight; it had made him conscious of something; that he was really meant for newspaper work, and it for him. He had a dim feeling of being at *home* in that office. He had intuitions of what the men were doing; the bits of talk he had heard, obscured though they were by newspaper dialect, sounded almost intelligible, sounded like a language which he must have spoken, centuries ago.

He walked along pondering this, and presently found himself in front of the fabled building of the Press. Some instinct guided him into the door; a queer pressure upon his brain, a sudden incomprehensible daring, made him go up the elevator and ask for the managing editor.

He sat down in an ante-room and under the eyes of an amused stenographer filled out a form: "Name," "age," "married" and "position desired." Under this last heading Josslyn wrote "editorial writer"; which seemed to be the only position suitable to a literary person.

After considerable delay a buzzer sounded at the desk of the stenographer, who said to Arthur: "Mr. Thain will see you now." Josslyn started. At the same instant the door opened, and a keen-faced youth, wearing an eye-shade and looking very angry, burst out, ignoring Josslyn, who slipped past him through the door.

At a large and badly scratched cherry-wood desk sat a bulky person about thirty years old (but looking older, Josslyn says), who wore spectacles and had a ruddy complexion, and looked quite as angry as the young man who had just gone out. He bent upon Arthur Josslyn a piercing and surprised stare. He looked at the filled-out form.

"What makes you think you could write editorials?" he demanded without preliminary.

"I don't know," Arthur replied.

The managing editor's mouth twitched. He flipped the form between his thick fingers, whistled gently and kept on staring at the limp but attentive young man before him.

"Supposing William D. Frost should drop dead on the street, what would you write about him?"

(Frost, Josslyn says, was then the most prominent banker in the city.)

The applicant hesitated. Had he known it, more than the mere question of writing editorials hung upon his answer. The truth was that Thain, a man of lightning impulses, had already made up his mind to hire Josslyn, not as an expert, but as a cub. He had seen in the youngster's face a sincerity, an alertness, even a power that he wanted to harness. Josslyn did not guess this; nor did he know that his answer to the question just put would reveal whether he was genuine; that if he tried a pretense of knowing about William D. Frsot he was doomed.

Well, Josslyn blushed fiery red (as he admits) and replied:

"I'm sorry. I never even heard that name."

Thain threw himself back in his chair and laughed, a bit triumphantly. Straightening up, he turned his spectacles once more upon Josslyn and said:

"Suppose you try reporting. Twelve a week to start."

The weird feeling that all this was familiar, that he had heard it all before, seized Josslyn again. Reporting! The word had dazzling suggestions, it had terrors, but it was delicious. He answered weakly:

"Ill try it."

He heard Thain call out: "Miss T——, take Mr. Josslyn to Mr. Franklin."

And the stenographer, more amused-looking than ever, conducted him to the youth with the eye-shade, and so into journalism.

[III]

FROM Happyville to the city; this was the leap Josslyn had made.

Imagine it. He did not know that justice is not only blind, but corrupt and often ghastly. He had never been told that politics, as then practiced in the city (if not now) was mainly a bestial struggle for salaried office, and that most politicians were degraded wire pullers, liars and thieves, who would stoop to anything, betray any kind of trust, to gain an advantage. He had never heard that criminals bought their freedom, that innocent men were hanged in order to fatten the records of prosecutors, that women were bought and sold by the police, that landlords let tenants rot in order to save a few dollars, that buildings were falsely constructed and that when they collapsed the victims were cheated out of damages. Those were only a few of the things he did not know— nor worry about. He liked the city. The moving processions of people and vehicles in the streets had an air of happiness. Rapidly he grew less timid. He held his head up and smiled at people, and they returned his smile.

Sometimes he was puzzled, sometimes shocked. But faithfully he repeated the Happyville motto "God's in His heaven," and at such times, high in the blue above the gigantic smoking buildings, up there beyond the tangles of wires and scaffolding and water-tanks, he fancied he could actually see God, serene in His heaven, disposing of matters to the ultimate advantage of everybody.

The Star mentioned this with a grimace.

[IV]

IN those days the city was considerably smaller. It had much the same landmarks; that is, the stock yards smoked over here, and the steel mills over there, and the tall buildings stood by the lake, and the river wound itself three ways, through extraordinary aisles of factories and warehouses. But there were great areas of land, now covered with apartment houses or flat roofs, which at that time were merely expanses of clay and chickweed, or bloomed with the black-eyed Susan and wild geranium, or were tousled with scrub oak trees. The city was a congeries of villages, swarming industrial villages, rather than a metropolis. The immense strides toward metropolitanism had not yet fairly begun. Nowhere was to be found that glossy, opulent appearance that so much of the city wears at present. The downtown buildings, for the most part, were only six or eight stories high, and fairly dingy. Outlying districts gave birth mainly to wooden residences, lining long, monotonous streets. Everything seemed temporary, neglected—and yet bursting with ambition.

Life was terrific. The great inrush of foreigners had reached a peak. The jargon of speech, the jostling of antagonistic races, the introduction of weird ethnic blends from the utmost corners of Europe, made the city continually more wonderful, but more terrible. Strange crimes, strange customs, made the daily page of the city's history a bizarre placard shocking to the staid, half-Puritan older residents, mainly of New England stock. Big conflicts and contrasts were everywhere; life was fought out in the open. Openly, aldermen stole streets and alleys, contractors grafted, bankers embezzled, foreigners pursued Old World feuds, railroads killed people at grade crossings, and blackmailers stole children. But the "decent element" was waging war on these things; and there were men who exposed the grafters and embezzlers, and hanged the murderers, and began the education of the foreigners. There, at the dawn of the new century, dwelt side by side the extremes of coarseness and refinement, ignorance and culture, generosity and greed.

Through the swarming streets, along the wooden sidewalks bordering these still-blooming prairies, down festering alleys, in and out of hospitals and morgues, went Arthur Josslyn in pursuit of news.

Sometimes another reporter would say to him: "What a hell-hole the city is, ain't it?" But Josslyn would reply, wondering, "I don't think it's so bad."

Usually he thought it was glorious. At least, it was thrillingly new. He began to recognize here and there signs that humanity has faults; but nothing, so far, destroyed his certainty that the majority of men were well-meaning. Naturally he discovered as much good as bad, and at this stage of his growth the good things—oh, such as a policeman saving a group of school-children from a runaway—made the greater impression upon him. Deep within him lay a love of people that softened in his eyes the brutal gestures of the city, and there burned steadily in him a flame of poetry that lit his spirit on his worst of days.

Lake ships, sullenly followed their tugs out into the white-caps of the lake; the scarlet flare of open furnaces at night; the wonderful rush of a long train over a viaduct; the boulevards, with their processions of vehicles under shade trees; the West Side blocks swarming with children, and a tall cathedral bell sending down its blessing; religious processions in the foreign quarters; an old, cupolaed mansion, brooding far back among maples; a glimpse of a tall spire, with the sunset on it—such things as these Josslyn took home with him from his daily rounds.

In the office he was a cub—a promising cub. No one knew that he loved everybody; although some did know that he scribbled verse. The Old Man heard about it, and remarked curtly to Franklin, "Break him in." It was done. His salary was advanced two dollars a week—and his leisure was reduced. He was hustled here; hustled there. No more reverie for him. He was sent out on impossible pursuits of impossible mysteries; compelled to ring hostile door-bells and freeze on inhospitable front porches; ask crude questions of scholarly spinsters; watch heartbroken women identify relatives at the county morgue; demand of berserk city officials the truth about their resignations; interview indignant college presidents about "freak" questions of the hour; travel mile after mournful mile upon street cars; freeze, starve, and keep hopeless vigils for news that did not happen; spend his own money to the last cent on assignments and receive censure for spending so much.

He was being "broken in." The appraisers had determined that he was metal. Week by week he was assaying higher value. But he remained essentially the same Josslyn.

[VI]

FROM this memoir and that, I can easily construct the scene of Josslyn's early endeavors. The news-room was in the same place, but it housed several departments since banished, and was crowded beyond belief. The Old Man spent his mornings there, growling and creaking at a desk by a window; his private office he used in the afternoons only. A good many of the reporters were denied desks, and did their typing on a low shelf that ran around the walls. There was hardly gangway. Toward press-time the noise must have been awful. Add to the staff numerous callers, who had no place to wait except among the desks; add especially the parasites of the sporting department, which had a turbulent corner of its own, and fancy it all! Three chairs near the sporting editor's desk were nearly always occupied by rising prize fighters, who glared, shuffled their feet, and spat. There was usually a group of press-agents telling someone foul stories.

In this place the gentle Josslyn began his career; writing his maiden stories upon a shelf, amid all that din, and with volleys of strange talk in his ears.

The staff was a rare mixture; it was "the pick of the town." There was Billy Fleming, immoral, witty, and pock-marked, a writer of ribald verse and graceful obituaries; Tom Griggs, the sad-eyed "police man," connoisseur of corpses and motives;

those two drunkards, Fox and Jones; "little Ed." Moore, a tramp reporter said to have been part Mexican; the debonaire Ernest Tripe, whose pay check was always drawn in advance; and various less memorable beings. A quaint, smeared, turbulent company of reprobates, full of fight and liquor, desperate in their pursuit of news, ignorant of all the modern "ethics of the profession," and clever as the devil himself. It must have taken months for Josslyn even to arrive on passable terms with them. I picture him laboring at his typewriter, trying to shape his stories according to the iron-bound model of the time, and conscious of the grins and whispers of those devils behind his back. I imagine him timorously submitting his copy to the fiery-tempered Franklin. I see him sitting silently in a corner, while the copy desk slaughtered his phrases. But still more vividly I vision him amid a group of those tobacco-spitting pirates, listening after hours to their memoirs, their theories, and their advice. For they did give him advice, I am sure. No doubt they were even kind to him. There is a sort of lofty and casual concern for the neophyte in the most abandoned and sophisticated of reporters. And besides, Josslyn always had a vein of good nature disarming to the cynic.

As for Franklin, he was gentle to his "cub." They saw quite a bit of each other, for they two were always the first to report in the morning;

and Franklin, groaning and cursing, would start slashing the morning paper with his long scissors, and would have Josslyn help him. One morning, Josslyn recalls, the city editor delivered this lecture from the corner of his mouth:

"Kid, I like your work, but you don't belong here. You're too sensitive. You're too well educated. . . . Gimme that pile of clippings. . . . Thanks. . . . Business'll kill you if you keep on. Look at me, hauled out of bed at five every morning; rush to my desk, stay there till last dog's hung. Fight, fight, fight, all the time. Fight with the staff, with the readers of the paper, with the town itself. Damn the town! It would get on anybody's nerves. . . . Get a quieter job, where you can write those poems of yours. Nothing in this boiler-shop grind. . . ."

The Old Man opened his door just then. Perhaps he had overheard some of the tirade, for that afternoon Franklin approached Josslyn and blurted:

"Don't take too seriously what I said this morning. I was sore at the world, that's all. You've got a nice style, and you'll get on in the business all right."

"Yes, sir," replied Josslyn, as he had learned to reply.

There could be no doubt that the Old Man prized Josslyn, in a way. He never spoke a word directly to him, and yet Josslyn had a singular feeling that he was watched, and not unkindly. More than once he suspected that the assignments Franklin gave him were inspired by the managing editor. On one occasion Josslyn was sent out of town with a group of aldermen "junketing" to New York. He muffed the assignment terribly, and returned to the office in a tremor. But nothing was said until the young reporter took courage to ask Franklin, "Just how badly did I fail on that trip?" The city editor pushed up his eye-shade, looked at Josslyn in his melancholy way, and said, gruffly, "It doesn't matter now. But I'll tell you if it had been anybody else the Old Man would have canned him without notice."

Whence arose this interest, this semi-benevolent interest, which Thain, formidable and ruthless being that he was, felt in the shrinking amateur? It was more unusual in those days than now, for it was said of the Old Man that when comparatively young he had "no favorites and no friends." He was a battler, like his creation Franklin, with his hand against the world. There is, though, no accounting for affections; and it was to be demonstrated that the Old Man loved Josslyn like a son; loved him at first sight, as one might say, rejoiced like any father at Josslyn's later success, and grieved like one when at last——

[VII]

AFTER he had been on the staff five years Josslyn was made city editor. Franklin in a burst of fury, had resigned. The Old Man said to Josslyn, "Take the desk, and let's see how long you can hold it." He did not reveal that he had offered the post to several of the older men, and that they had excused themselves. Josslyn, elate, apprehensive, the most competent of them all but the most humble, took the desk.

A good many of the piratical crew still remained. After having been Josslyn's comrades and critics, they now found themselves his subordinates. There was no complaint. They regarded Josslyn with that curious mixture of respect, pity, and disdain which they would have shown toward any other city editor. ("Little Ed" Moore said: "I was offered the job, but my God! d'ye think I'd take it? Under the Old Man?"). They liked Josslyn. They rallied about him—good old pirate crew. Perhaps the assignments he gave them were not always to their taste; no matter, they covered these assignments and stolidly wrote the results. Perhaps Josslyn made mistakes in orders, charted the wrong course. The old hands merely left the office humming, and got the news after their own fashion. There grew up a warm loyalty to Josslyn. He had lost none of his gentility during the years of reporting. He could always see the other fellow's side of an argument. Often he forgave a man when he got drunk. Often when the Old Man told him to discharge such-and-such a scapegrace, Josslyn forgot to discharge him.

In the meantime he found that, having served one apprenticeship, he was now serving another. He was being "broken in" again. Not so much now by contact with the city and its people, but by the mechanisms of the office, by the emergencies of his work, by the thousands of shocks and griefs that went with responsibility. The comparative ease of mind that is the underling's only recompense for being an underling began to leave him. The little flame of interest with which he used to await his morning assignment was now denied. He awoke each day quivering with prescience of what he must face. No day was ever the same as its predecessor. No problem ever arose in precisely the same guise. The incalculable world prepared for Josslyn incalculable emergencies and pitfalls. Glory and disgrace both lay in wait for him at his desk. He was satisfied to escape disgrace. He was satisfied to end the day without a reprimand from the Old Man, or without some failure too abject even for comment. He was alternately elate with hope and smothered in shame. He was a poet compelled to face a despot —and to be one.

This growing torment received a new complication when he moved to a suburb. It was a charming suburb, more beautiful than Happyville;

a forest spot, with great elms overshadowing the streets, and with the children of the forest, ferns, flowers and wild creatures, still occupying the glades. Fanny, the sister, had insisted upon moving thither from the city flat. The change improved Josslyn's physical health, but the country drew away a lot of the affection and confidence that he had bestowed upon the city. In its high seasons, with its gorgeous flowerings, it made the city hideous by contrast; and at its saddest of times it had a repose, a sanity, that made Josslyn more and more regretful to leave it, even for a few hours. Sunday afternoons and holidays came to be colored with regret and foreboding; regret that so perfect tranquillity could not be kept just a little longer; foreboding of the new plunge, tomorrow, into chaos.

He knew it to be chaos, even though he tasted there a bitter intoxicant. Born newspaper man though he was, carried beyond himself by news, subject to all the ecstasies of that weird and perishable form of experience, there was still his temperament, one-half of which craved peace, craved even more the expression of the wistful poetry in him. He managed somehow to strangle these more feminine impulses while he was busy with the affairs of "the desk"; that is, for all those years he managed to do so. But though strangled, they were not dead, and they often confused him, rising before his eyes at inopportune times. The Old Man was keen to detect these waverings in his young city editor. He seemed to sense them out while sitting in his room. Presently he would appear, perhaps clutching a copy of an opposition paper.

"Scooped again! Really, Josslyn . . . Didn't you have this affair down in the assignment book? Well, how can you expect to cover advance dates without putting them down? Depend on your memory; is that it? . . . Well, for goodness' sake, get a little of the thing written for the last Final."

Exit, with his shoulders high.

Or this:

"Josslyn, I must have a talk with you. I'm doing my best to build you up into an efficient newspaper man. Sometimes I think you'll never make it. Sometimes I think you're writing those —er—pesky poems, in your head. Come out of it. Poetry'll get you nowhere."

"I'm not writing poetry, Mr. Thain."

"Well, if it isn't poetry, it's love. If you're in love, for God's sake, get married. That's the only cure. And get a blonde; they're safer."

He would follow this with things that would make Josslyn blush. Josslyn believes the Old Man liked to see him blush. Thain was, no doubt, puzzled and plagued by this temperament, which partly mocked him with what he himself had been, and partly eluded his analysis. He always posed before Josslyn as a bitter cynic, pagan, hater of all religions, and defier of all conventions. He usually held up to the youth a harsh, sordid conception of life, and a stern view of journalism, which he said was an exact science. This was his way of "building up a spine in the fellow"; and it worked—for a good while. But we all think that, while he was administering the bitter tonic, he laughed strangely in private. He was cute. Once when he and Josslyn had worked together preparing a tremendously hot story, and Josslyn was just leaving the stone, collarless and with flying hair, the Old Man spoke a loud aside to Big Jim, the foreman: "There goes a great newspaper man." Intend Josslyn to overhear it? Surely. And he knew, of course, that the young man would carry away that immense compliment with him, and that the yeast would work and work; and that, for a week at least, it would fill him with a sense of high enterprise.

But it was the Old Man's weakness at that period that he grimly refused to know anything about the private lives of his staff. So he knew nothing about Josslyn's house, or about his flowers. And he did not know that, when walking home in the evening along the elm-shaded streets of the village, Josslyn looked back with vague disgust upon what he had done.

He was conscious only of a grey retrospect, out of which some incidents stood sharply; incidents whose effect upon his inner structure he did not fully understand. Such as—well, such as the story of an old murder trial dug up twenty years late to confront the innocent children of the forgotten murderer. Complaint from the widow. Reference of complaint to the Old Man. Josslyn exonerated. A feeling of regret, tempered by elation over having scooped the Journal.

Or such as the publication of a wrong picture; the picture of the twin brother of an accused thief. Twin brother a grocer. Grocery ruined. The wrong twin writes misspelled letter, hinting at libel suit. Josslyn sends Griggs, the paper's best "fixer," to settle the matter. Griggs settles it for seventy-five dollars. Immense relief on the part of Josslyn; coupled with scruples.

Moral complexities, these. They don't, after all, get to the bottom of Josslyn. There at the bottom was his instinct to bestow affection, to condone, to work for the happiness of everybody. Now this is impossible in an executive. He must decide sharp issues, and always someone gets hurt. Let there be a dispute between a reporter and a copy reader. Josslyn must decide it somehow. Someone injured. Both men dear to him. Someone must subside, with a flushed face and a biting of lips, and, looking at him, Josslyn is wretched. Perhaps he decided wrongfully. He takes the doubt home with him.

Josslyn told the Star that of all things most abhorrent to him were the quarrels. Next to this, the eternal naggings about salaries. The requests for increases had to go to the Old Man for decision, but they always came to Josslyn first.

The symptoms? Josslyn tells them with a shudder.

A reporter or copy reader comes to "the desk" after the First Final has gone. He hovers at the desk. The appeal in his eye is unmistakable.

"Well, John."

"Ahem. . . . . . I've been working here almost two years now, Mr. Josslyn. . . I . . ."

"It's about your salary, I suppose."

"Yes, sir; that's it." (At other times he may call Josslyn "A. J.," but now it is "sir.") He goes on: "I thought maybe you wouldn't mind speaking to the Old Man about me."

A pause. Josslyn is fairly sick He looks down at his desk, twiddles his pencil, and says: "I'll do what I can, John."

The poor, hang-dog chap, the work-worn, bankrupt ne'er-do-well, brightens pitifully. Ah, but Josslyn is sorry for him! A "raise"? Josslyn would give him a doubled, a trebled salary. Josslyn starts to speak, but gulps it back. He must not "commit himself". John the reporter goes away, whistling.

That's all. Just things like that. Nothing at all to an iron man, such as an executive ought to be. Executives should sit at desks, full of blood and confidence, and shoot back defiant things when people make requests. And they ought to go home with hearty step, certain they have done right, and with some such thought as "Greatest editor of greatest paper on earth; 's what I am."

Lots of them do.

[VIII]

PICTURE Josslyn on a tranquil spring morning, going to work with the sweetness of flowers in his nostrils, with the budding trees whispering to him a mood of peace. And then suppose him entering the office and being greeted by: "Boss, there's a four-eleven fire in the Yards. Six bodies taken out. It's been burning since six o'clock. What shall we do?" Or, "The bureau has just 'phoned Marshall Field is dying. Shall I get somebody started with the obit? Who do you want to go up to the house?" Or picture him with big news "breaking" and three of his best men sick. Or suppose him quietly opening his morning mail and finding in it a notice of a $100,000 libel suit. Or fancy him starting to close his desk at night, and picking up a rival to discover a triumphant "beat." Or consider him a moment when griefs are in a lull, when he gazes about the office in reverie, and then —— a voice at his desk, the voice of his best reporter: "Boss, I'm sorry, but I've got a better offer from the Globe. I'm leaving Saturday."

Reader, not of the profession, these things mean little to you. But to Josslyn every one of these surprises, these threats or disappointments, contains poison. And for our Josslyn every one was magnified by his imagination. Was he "scooped?" He saw the black type of his rival dancing jigs upon the news-stands, he saw thousands grasping for the story missing in so ghastly fashion from the Press, he imagined a murmur of comment on the streets, in the trains, and himself skulking in by-ways. Was he sued? He previsioned a stern jury handing down the verdict of thousands, the Old Man frantic, the paper bankrupt, himself outcast, the city pointing a huge collective finger.

But correspondingly vivid his triumphs. Ah, yes! to conquer them all, to breathe deeply for a moment over what he and his men had done— even Josslyn's nature had rich delights over that. Delights lasting sometimes an hour or two. Then the dark cloud of premonition, the goad of new emergencies. Into it again. "Josslyn, Moore on the 'phone; murder in Little Hell——"

And the great clock upon the wall, never stopping never relenting; the clock that makes slaves of us all. . . .

Despite everything, he grew. Certain motions and mental processes became automatic. His adjustment to the swift and deadly requirements of his job became easier. The shrinking, apprehensive Josslyn still dwelt in him, but over this seemed to grow another personality with an apparent defiance of disaster. Long ago it had become unnecessary for the older men to tell him what to do; they now respectfully sought his judgment. It began to be whispered about that he was "one of the best city editors in town." The slim body and the gentle, sensitive mind had seemingly withstood the efforts of fate, the Old Man and the devil to crush them. And not only the office, but the city itself and all it could send lay at Josslyn's feet. The great city roared about him, challenging him with its brutal voices, preparing for him sudden horrors, ringing his telephone with the message: "Ah,—ha, Josslyn! See what's happened now." But he seemed to be a match for the city. Nothing it could do but would find him ready. With a stroke he could turn its challenges and fierce taunts, its outbursts, the jets from its caldrons, to serve the paper. And, daily, he seemed to grow calmer. The boys said he was "hard-boiled." Josslyn, the master! Well, well!

Then one day he went in to the Old Man and said: "Mr. Thain, I'll have to stop. I'll have to give up the city desk. It's got the best of me. I——I just can't——"

And Josslyn fainted away, right there on the Old Man's Brussels rug.

The Old Man and the office boy raised him to an old lounge in the "private room," and they inexpertly poured water on him, and the staff gathered around. I was there myself. I shall never forget the quaint surprised tenderness with which the Old Man gazed, blinking, upon his downfallen greyhound of a city editor, and how he said, oratorically: "My Lord, I guess a six months' vacation won't be too much for this boy . . . . The best city editor I ever . . . . He's just simply done himself."

But when Josslyn opened his eyes, this speech changed to: "Billy, fetch a cab . . . . You, sir, go home and take a hot drink. The rest of you, why the devil aren't you working?"

[IX]

JOSSLYN, grey man of the copy desk, do you think of those days? Can you remember how the telephone spoke to you, straight from the fierce heart of the city, and how you used to say to us, with a slap on the shoulder, and such a light in your eyes, "Go after it, old chap; go after it and get it?" And do you remember days of tension, of waiting and waiting; and how as we all sat there waiting, the Great Event would at last "break?" Josslyn, those days of anxiety, strain, effort, accomplishment, gladness, when you were the leader of us all! And, Josslyn, those afternoons when we would hang about your desk when the paper was out, and bring smiles to your face with our banter. And how sweet it was, when the city could do no more to us for a few hours, to put on our coats and go out—free!—into the streets, lighting our pipes. Those tremendous years, Josslyn, when you were the Boss, and life was vivid. Remember, Josslyn, grey creature writing head-lines?

Josslyn

PART TWO

[I]

T WOULD have surprised anyone unacquainted with newspaper offices to hear how little stir the break-down of the city editor of the great Press caused in our news-room. There is a special optimism—or perhaps a special callousness—for such cases. It is based upon the knowledge that, no matter who falls, the army always advances, the machine never stops. And then, we have seen so many men "blow up," fall ill, or go crazy, that when something happens we merely look sympathetic and wait until the patient is cured.

Naturally it did seem a little strange, the next morning after Josslyn's collapse, to hear George Brown coolly say into Josslyn's telephone:

"He isn't here. He's sick. Anything I can do for you?"

And it did impress us queerly when we walked up to take assignments from Brown and had to say "yes, sir" to a comrade with whom we had wrangled the day before on equal terms. But this feeling wore off. Presently we were used to Brown, with his cool, abrupt manner; and barring a vague sense of loss—the lack of some intangible, supporting presence—we breasted our tasks the same as ever.

There was plenty of talk, certainly. It fed upon the fact that we were cautioned not to go to Josslyn's home, nor even to call him on the telephone. A rumor started that he was dying; but this was exploded by someone who had seen him walking with his sister. Then the melodramatic stories gave way to an assurance that he was only taking a "good long rest." And by and by the word came officially from the Old Man's room that Josslyn was going to Europe. Promptly after this announcement, Josslyn reappeared in the office. He was thin and somewhat silent; but he was whole. I recall that we gave him a "banquet," which would have been desperately dull had not the Drunkard (then on his first term of service) arrived intoxicated and made all the speeches. Josslyn himself had little to say. He sat at the head of the table fingering his fork, and with a wistful look in his eyes. The affair broke up at nine o'clock. We forgot to tip the waiters.

[II]

HE WENT to London to "investigate industrial conditions." From there he crossed to Paris, without having cabled a word.

I return now to what I have learned through my proxy, the Star. Without him I never should have got so close to Josslyn's memories of Paris, nor should I be able to set down almost word for word Josslyn's terse, but eloquent picture of the Beautiful City:

Paris from the Butte of Montmartre: A labyrinth of slums, watched over by the Basilica, slums in which foulness and poetry dwell side by side, and beyond which rises Paris quivering in the vapor from myriad chimneys. Brown masses of buildings, blending into the lavender shadows of the surrounding hills; mysterious cloud-shapes of roofs, from which loom the towers of Notre Dame and St. Sulpice, the dome of the Invalides, the peaks, tiny in perspective, of great houses once imperial.

Paris from the region of the Trocadero; at one's feet the river; then the armored limbs of the Eiffel Tower, spanning a broad promenade; then the dwindling harmony of buildings and the wistful horizon. Belated sunbeams drift over the Trocadero hill, tingeing the river with pink, touching with slow fire the windows of houses lining the river in its curve toward the northeast. Far away, a flash, perhaps from the golden lions of the Pont Alexander III.

Paris of the Champs Elysees; Paris from the Arc de Triomphe: That thrilling downward sweep of pearly "hotels," veteran chestnut trees, and avenue. The finger of the obelisk, poised against the distant color-splashes of the Tuileries. Beauty after the manner of the Bourbons and Bonapartes. Sublimity created by a sweep of the scepter.

Paris of the Grand Boulevard: Buildings lacy with gilt-lettered signs; windows flashing with jewelry, perfumes, costumes, pictures; writhing masses of people in gaudy uniforms or gaudier gowns; arc-lights quivering red and yellow by night and conveying their tints to the languid tree-branches; tides of people chattering, murmuring, shuffling; streams of motors, clashing, hooting; cafes roaring, sparkling. A mild, indulgent moon sailing over all.

Paris of the "left bank": Crooked, tatterdemalion streets, concealed convent gardens, slim, monocled studios, crack-brained huddles of roofs, mansards, ruins; churches rotting behind hoardings; dim by-ways, green lanterns on the corners; gurgles of laughter and music.

Paris of the Seine: The essence of what is loveliest and most mysterious in the Beautiful City. Below there, below the parapet, "she" glides. (The Seine is always "elle" to the Parisian.) "She" glides by, rapid but solemn, infatuated with herself. She wears satin, shading from blue to black. "She" hurries under bridges, drifts reverently past Notre Dame, boils proudly past the Chambre des Deputes. And the grey houses seem to bend over, Narcissus-like, to gaze into the passionate stream.

No one can look back without emotion upon these and manifold other things one has seen in Paris. The Bautiful City lies there behind, a receding spectacle, an interlude in the imperative rhythm of life, to most people a memory like a passing love affair.

Such a memory remains still in Josslyn's mind, but blurred by his misery—for he was miserable. He remembers journeys, conversations, meager errands and half-hearted literary work of that strange period. A few faces peer out spectrally from the fog; a few glimpse of the beauty and vivacity of the amazing capital remains with him, strangely woven with black moods when he was all but casting himself into the Seine. And there was one day when he walked in the Luxembourg, by accident, with France Herself; a girl of the quarter who pitied him, spoke caressingly to him, and nearly tempted him to fall in love with her, and remain in Paris for life.

The Star smiled his wisest smile at this point in his narrative.

"You should have seen," said he, "how the good old fellow blinked when he let slip that glimpse of his European experience. He shut himself up quickly and switched to a description of Parisian streets. And then he told me of a day he spent on Montmartre hill, looking down over the magic city, and imagining a leap into Hell. A different sort of Hell from being city editor. This would be a complete abandonment of duty, of effort, of morals. It would be easy, he fancied, to walk down into that valley of beckoning arms and gaudy carnival and simply disappear. In a few weeks or days, he would be buried under the tide of pleasure. He would get drunk, and stay drunk. He would cast anchor at Maxim's or the Hole in the Wall, would hurl the last of his expense money upon the table, and would swim in the prismatic flood of booze until he sank. And at last, exhausted, he would be cast upon some desolate urban beach, finished, drowned."

Over and over, the Star tells me, this temptation came to Josslyn. It would have been a cheerful ending, would it not, to the history of a specially constructed optimist? Yet as one reviews our friend's mental struggle, such a crisis as he passed through seems inevitable. To be bred in the belief that the world is altogether a safe and beautiful place, to be shielded from the sorry pageantry of cities, and then to have suddenly spread before his eyes the real thing, is a shock that would unsettle any intellect. There is nothing new about it. It has happened to any number of scholars, and to innumerable honest theological students. It has even happened to newspaper men. The majority of these last, however, are able to shield their feelings in professional unconcern.

Their flashes of sympathy, though genuine, are brief. They go home laughing, shutting off instinctively the hideous kinetoscope of the day.

Now it may be guessed that on that day of his fainting fit there had broken down in Josslyn—at least for a while—the last supports of his faith that "God's in His heaven." Physical depression was piled upon mental. It had been a terrible day, anyhow. I forgot to mention that it was "Black Friday," when murderers are hanged. Always the worst of all days for Josslyn; always days of strain, of mental torment, of pity, and of anger. Everything culminated in his collapse, which had been preparing for weeks under his poise; the collapse of his beliefs, his self-confidence, and his sense of authority.

There would have been no use making suggestions to the Old Man, but Europe was not the place for Josslyn. Beside some peaceful lake, near home, he might have recovered the illusions of Happyville, at least in some degree. In Europe he absorbed poisons from which he did not recover. In that new and intoxicating atmosphere, alone among thousands of fatalistic and indifferent people, he listened to the messages that lead to madness; the messages: "Do what you like; go to Hell if you like; who cares?"

Imagine him lying awake in his hotel room in the Latin Quarter, and thinking, thinking, thinking. Should he ever go back? If so, to what?

He is a failure. At home he has collapsed; collapsed shamefully. Here he is supposed to write things, and he cannot write them. He is adrift, lost. He is quite as aimless as those drunkards, or drug fiends, howling in the streets . . . . How they howl! There is a woman who always comes through Josslyn's street about midnight, shrieking prayers, or curses . . . . One cannot understand her. There is a sound of crashing boards down at the wine-shop on the corner. There is a scurrying of feet; a flurry of insane laughter . . .

Paris is full of weird sounds. Its bells are mournful. The clatter of its carts and tram-wheels among the silent stone houses is strange. Locomotive whistles have a piercing, puny, fading note, terribly distressing. Eerie voices hover among the mansards.

Josslyn is all alone, thinking, wondering.

Perhaps he goes upon the boulevards, there to mingle with slow-moving promenaders, all—he thinks—wearing a fatalistic grimace, an expression of "Do what you like; who cares?" In cafes he sees throngs of people leaning over little tables, people of all nationalities and types, mingled in feverish carouse. And in the streets there is a continuous, maddening tinkle, toot and swish, which compared with the good-natured roar of Josslyn's own city is like a crack-brained circus.

"Gay" Paris! Josslyn thought it sad. The lavishness, the brilliant, the hoydenishness, the "who cares?" of it all, smote him with a fancy that he was sliding with it to a soft, sickening death.

And there was always the thought seeping into his mind—maybe a transmission of thought from the boulevardiers—"You have lived long enough; worked long enough. Rest and play here. Go on to death with us. There's nothing in success. There's no effort worth while. Work is a fetich, and results—pooh, there are none!"

Sometimes he got out his portable typewriter and wrote in his room; wrote things that started sanely enough, and trailed off always into mere words. He threw away these writings. He never sent a line from Europe. This is why the legend of Josslyn's "trip abroad" has always been, in the news-room, an illustration of failure. His adventure has been unfavorably compared with the odysseys of Sinful Goode, and the sage remark always added: "It takes a certain type of man to do foreign service." This was what was meant in that cigar-store conversation, away back there.

I am glad to tell the truth as the Star learned it from Josslyn.

[III]

IN the office, I recall, there had begun to be murmurs and rumors again. Murmurs because— oh, we were merely human!—we didn't think "a man should be kept on the pay roll indefinitely, loafing in Europe." And there was considerable wonder because Josslyn didn't write to us. Not so much as a post-card. Campbell, who had the Old Man's ear, carefully sounded him for news. There was none. Josslyn hadn't written to the Old Man himself. But Campbell obtained the mail address of the absentee, and we all wrote to him. We gave him the latest news of the news-room; how Barlow had sprained his ankle, and Wade was doing make-up; how Old Slater had finally quit; how O'Toole, the photographer, had blown up the chancel of a church with his flash-light. Then we waited for a cheerful, brotherly answer from Josslyn. None came.

One day, quite unexpectedly, we learned that he was coming home. The rumor ran in no time from news-room to composing room; from composing room to cigar store. "Josslyn's coming back." Brown added the detail: "And darn glad I'll be to hand over his job." The office buzzed with honest pleasure. We liked Brown—but we wanted Josslyn.

Now bulletins began coming in earnest. He had sailed. He had reached New York. He was starting westward by twenty hour train. He was well.

We collaborated in a telegram: "Welcome home, Boss. The city is pickling hell for you."

It was astonishing how much we talked about this trifling matter, the return of Josslyn to the news-room; and also, how vividly we remembered things about him. The figure that had for a while been lost, that had become blurred by absence and preoccupation, now lived again before us, quiet, steady, and winsome. And we realized that we had, inwardly, given up ever seeing him again. We had accepted, in our fatalistic way, an unspoken suspicion that he had left the paper forever. Now there was no doubt of his return.

But no one should believe that we said things such as I have written. No, the things said among the desks were like this:

(From Brown) "I hope he's feeling strong and ugly. I'm going to tell him what I think of this lazy gang."

(From Barlow) "I'll take my vacation soon as he gets here. Got it all fixed, boys."

(From Wade) "I'm going to put in my application for a trip abroad. If he can go, I can."

(From the staff generally) "Soon as he gets back, watch me strike for my raise. "They've stalled me long enough."

It was not until much later that it was learned that the Old Man had ordered Josslyn back; ordered him back in three preemptory words.

It is only now that I am able to reveal—as those pompous foreign correspondents say—that the Old Man's cable reached Josslyn just as he was writing a letter of resignation from the staff.

[IV]

THE STAR has passed on to me Josslyn's description of his homeward journey; of how he paced the deck, gazed out over limpid seas, and flung away, bit by bit, the saffron fancies of his sick time; how he wept when he entered New York harbor; how he rushed home, with his face glued to the car-window, gulping in every detail of the American landscape. He could not sleep. The night hours he spent in the smoking-compartment, thinking, thinking, and adjusting himself anew to the city, the office, the men; trying to remember their faces; knowing that all that he cared for was there, in the news-room.

The city drew near. The shoulders of sand-dunes rose against the pale sky; they gave way to groups of wooden roofs, then to isolated, enormous factory buildings, and to flocks of chimneys. Silent, stolid, trains of freight-cars, oil-tanks, coal-barges, slid past. Tall cranes appeared, gigantic, foolish. Presently chimneys and roofs blended into masses. A narrow river was crossed, reflecting in its murky waters the masts of steamers. A brief rush through a valley of narrow streets, and there appeared the great, ghostly bodies of the steel mills, wrapped in ruby clouds of smoke. More streets; long, straight streets, wheeling by; a tall spire, like a monument; glimpses of parks and boulevards; then renewed chaos, upended bridges, mournful limbs and shoulders of factories, and enormous, monotonous assemblages of freight cars.

And at last he was among buildings fifteen stories tall, and taller; buildings with dazzling batteries of windows reflecting the morning sun. From among them rose, to surprise him, the slim, graceful body of a new hotel, with white stone facings, and the peaks of many another new landmark. Above rose the old characteristic clouds of smoke; and he could hear familiar voices, earsplitting sounds, mysterious mechanical wails and groans. It was his own city again, his own brilliant, challenging, fascinating but fearsome city. He looked upon its huge stone masses and its radiance of a million windows with a heightened pulse, and yet with a sort of despair. He had forgotten that it was all so gigantic. He had forgotten its tremendous impact.

On the way to the office new fears shook him; new certainty that he was a failure. No question, it was all gone, all that buoyancy with which he had endured the city desk, and defied the city itself.

When he reached the office, what should he do? He did not know.

[V]

WE had wired: "The city's pickling hell for you." And in fact, it had done just about that.

Events had started with a little strike of wholesale grocery clerks. Overnight, this petty grievance had swollen into a walkout of truck teamsters; and before anybody could catch his breath all the "Jehus" had laid down the reins and swarmed into the streets to make trouble. The owners had sworn defiance, and had sent out wagons, manned by gloomy-looking drivers and by two policemen apiece, to "break the strike." The usual result: chaos. On the day we telegraphed Josslyn our welcome, wagons were being crippled and burned in various places about town, and isolated reports were coming in of strike-breakers being stoned and chased down alleys. On the next day the down-town district was just one solid riot. Caravans of guarded wagons were being driven through the main streets; and the sidewalks were pre-empted by mobs that followed these wagons with imprecations, and worse. Right in front of the city hall bricks flew like chaff; a stray revolver shot broke a window in the mayor's office; a patrol wagon was tipped over.

In front of our office, that day about ten o'clock, the trouble came to a head. The mob concentrated in the narrow street under our windows, and there was a tempest of shooting, shouts, and unexplained crashes. Across the street we could see the windows full of people, some merely gazing curiously down, but others, I regret to say, throwing ink-stands, chair-legs, and other missiles down upon the police. One group of young devils on a fire-escape poured boiling water on the back of a team of horses, which proceeded to dash into the crowd and mow down a few innocent by-standers. Half of the staff was at the windows, enjoying the spectacle, while the other half wrote descriptions like mad, or scrawled head-lines for extras. People ran about yelling above the awful noise that came in from the street. And at his big desk Brown, with his collar off and his shirt open at the neck, jumped up and down and side-wise, trying to write "leads," answer telephones, and say "Yes, sir; yes, sir" to the Old Man, all with the same motion.

Into this bedlam suddenly came Josslyn.

We had almost forgotten him. Nobody had had any time to gossip, to busy himself with absentees. So Josslyn came in as though it were out of the blue, instead of out of that murderous street. I recall that he slipped in at the door of the newsroom, pretty quietly, set down his suit-case, and drew his handkerchief across his forehead. A boy, vaulting for the door with copy, nearly upset his old Boss and never looked to see who it was. One of the desk-men looked up and smiled. And Josslyn just stood there, seeming a bit dazed and out of place.

Pretty soon Brown had a breathing-space, bit a piece from an unlit cigar and whirled around to find the rightful owner of his desk standing there. George jumped up with a "Well!" He held out his hand, but just then his private telephone buzzed, and he leaped to answer it. Josslyn, halted midway of a greeting, looked more taken aback than ever. He caught sight of me, and his eyes took on that affectionate light that was so natural to them; but he did not come forward. He hung there by the door, with the strangest, timid, baffled manner. I noticed now that he was more carefully dressed than he used to be, and that there was an odd deliberateness about his movements.

The staff, by now, was beginning to wake up to his presence. Two or three of the men started up to shake hands, and a couple of new chaps standing near me whispered "That's Josslyn, used to be city editor, you know." There might have been quite a reception in a minute or two, had it not been for the entrance of the Old Man. He came in at long strides, and with a furious frown, and with his hands full of proofs. Josslyn heard him coming, and stepped to one side, and the Old Man brushed by him heedlessly, his old specks flashing sparks.

"Look here, Brown, what do you mean by this . . . . " was the beginning of the sentence he left trailing in his path as he went by. There was a buzz and clatter around the city desk for five minutes, during which we by-standers kept our noses on our copy-reading or clattered our typewriters dutifully. When I looked up from work Josslyn had disappeared.

That was all until afternoon, when I was told there was something going on in the composing room. I went out, and found a ring of printers and editors gathered about the stone, from which the last forms of the First Final had just been slid to the stereotypers. The gang stood about with grins and great brawny arms folded; smeary faced "galley boys" hung nearby, open-mouthed. Big Jim, the foreman, was making a speech to somebody. Through the ring I could just see the slim form and quiet face of Josslyn. The face was not only quiet; it was tired; and it was dejected. He stood there with a sort of wistful smile, a bashful shadow of a smile, his mouth quivering with—well, I wouldn't swear that it was a smile at all. And Big Jim was making a speech of welcome, working in all the old bromides and stale jokes appropriate to such an event. Josslyn was always a tremendously popular man with the printers.

Going back into the hall, I met Brown just coming out of the Old Man's room. He seized me by the shoulder, mysteriously.

"Look here," he said. "Don't tell anybody just yet; but Josslyn isn't coming back to the desk."

He looked such a combination of ruefulness and elation that I almost laughed.

"You're keeping the job, then?" I asked.

"Yes." We looked at each other, both thinking of that figure, so like and yet so unlike our Josslyn of old, who was being toasted at the stone.

"The Old Man says," Brown murmured confidentially, "the Old Man says Josslyn is afraid to take the desk again. Lost his nerve, he says. I don't mean to tell anyone but you. Looks as though I was knocking my predecessor, don't you see? But, Harry, the gist of it is, Josslyn is through . . . . Well, I must look after the late Final."

[VI]

WAS it fair to say he had "lost his nerve?" You may judge from the interview as I have it through the Star.

They were together in the Old Man's room, with the door shut. The Old Man had done Josslyn the honor to get out of his chair and shake hands with him.

They looked into each other's faces, and they concealed as best they could the affection born years before, and always invulnerable to quarrels.

And the Old Man said:

"I've been thinking—you ought to have another assistant. The paper's been growing. Job's too much for one man and a greenhorn . . . By the way, I've been using your old desk sometimes. You can have it back."

Josslyn made no reply. He sat staring at the floor.

The Old Man wiped his glasses and went on, with a change of mood:

"That crowd out there . . . . need somebody to

take hold of 'em. Brown's all right, but too calm; too calm. I can't shout at 'em all the time. I'm getting old, Josslyn."

This could go no further. Josslyn said:

"Mr. Thain, please don't make plans—I can't go back to the city desk."

The Old Man almost dropped his glasses. However, he managed to put them on, very cautiously, and he favored Josslyn with one of his heavy looks.

"I presume," he remarked at length, "that this is one of your temperamental days. I remember you used to have 'em. Poetry, poetry! . . . Well, that's all past and gone. You can't fool me, kid."

"No, Mr. Thain, I assure you that I——"

"Assure me of nothing. You are city editor. Tomorrow you take hold of the desk and the assignment book. I——we understand each other. Been on the job too many years. I want you, first of all, to give the pay-roll a good winnowing. It'll stand it."

Josslyn rose. (I am giving this exactly as he told it to the Star.)

"Mr. Thain——I'm sorry. You've always been more than good to me."

His voice broke. He admits it.

"Don't be a baby!" The Old Man was furious. He was beginning to believe Josslyn now, and he was frightened—and grieved. "Don't blubber. Just look the thing over. In the first place I taught you the business. I built up a spine in you, inch by inch. I—damn you—I half killed you, but I made you. Now you come back here, and you think you can slip out from under. No, sir! I say you can't. You can't treat me like that. No human being would stand it."

Josslyn was silent.

"There," went on the Old Man more mildly, "you begin to see the point, don't you? Why, kid, it wouldn't stand to reason that you would pass me up, any more than I would pass you up. We've been through too much together."

He waited.

Josslyn said: "You don't suppose I want to leave the paper? I wasn't thinking of that. I don't want to quit . . . I want a job writing, or something . . . I can't go back to the desk."

The Old Man thrust his hands in his pockets, and leaned back in his chair. His face, Josslyn, says, was a study in injured dignity, perplexity, and wrath. But his eyes, when he turned them Josslyn's way, had a softer glint, somehow. Was it possible he was thinking of his own disappointments; of his own ambitions of years ago, when very likely he had said the same thing to somebody; that he wanted to be a writer, and not an executive?

But his voice came cold.

"We don't need any writers. We need hard-boiled editors."

"Well, then, Mr. Thain, I resign."

The Old Man glared, opened his mouth, but held his peace.

"How about the copy-desk?" asked Josslyn, after three minutes of ghastly silence.

"Talk to George Brown," snapped the Old Man. "He's the city editor."

It was the beginning of his new relationship with Josslyn, his relation of frigid business, shorn of all personal touch.

It was the end of the great interview, of which we knew so little at the time, and about which Josslyn has never talked until the Star got it out of him.

It was the beginning of Josslyn's final phase—for he will never have another, in this news-room.

[VI]

COMPREHENDING him now, I sometimes watch this comrade at his work, and think: "After all, is his fate so deplorable?" I think also: "After all, perhaps the outcome was best for everyone."

George Brown is city editor. He is built for it. Brown never falters, never doubts. He gives orders and administers discipline with a fine air He assails difficulties with quivering nostrils; downs them, then laughs. There are few complexities about Brown. It is ordained that he shall have men under him like Josslyn; that Josslyn, a finer, keener spirit, shall take orders from a man who never has wavered, as he himself wavered. "Josslyn, read this quick, will you?" "Hurry that eight-column line, Josslyn." "I say, Josslyn, do the make-up today, will you?" "Or, "Here's a problem, Josslyn; what do you make of it?" Josslyn? Why he can do anything; knows all about the business. They say that he knows the initials of every prominent citizen; that his mind is stored with useful details of past events; that he can locate a classical quotation unerringly; and that he can tell you the capitals of even the French colonies in Africa.

He isn't anybody; only Josslyn.

Well, then, shall we conclude that he is soured, despondent, or bitter? Surely, we know him too well to think that he is. The despair that seized him ten years ago, the violent negation of his youthful trust, the urge to taste death and Hell, are gone. Ten years of quiet work at his profession have wrought a cure. He takes life now without frenzies, without eagerness or illusions. He is not to be fooled by ignes fatui; nor is he to be terrorized by scare-crows.

For him, it has settled down to this: He will face what comes, and do what offers; and always, always, he will bear himself in this news-room so as to encourage gladness and assuage unhappiness. Titles, distinctions, jurisdiction — empty words, all.

He will be the best man he can in his little circle of the world; the masters of larger circles are welcome to them.

This, if you please, is his Career.

{XIII}
The Late Watch
[I]

IX O'CLOCK, and all's well. The watch changes.

It has become dark by a slow dropping of shade into the valley where our building squats among sky-scrapers. Lights burn in the news-room; one illumines the city desk, others, widely scattered among patches of darkness, beam casually upon other desks. The day is really done. But the day is stretching itself into a night.

Six o'clock. The Old Man, like a true sentinel, thrusts his head in at the door, and perceives that all is well. He wears a new and handsome derby and is pink with barbering. He is going out, one suspects. His glasses twinkle.

"Good-night, Josslyn."

"Good-night."

The Old Man takes a step into the room.

"You'd better go to dinner soon. Dunstane can watch the 'phone while you're out . . . . A child could let go the dummy anyhow . . . I doubt if he'll die before morning."

Josslyn appears to understand these cryptic sentences. He stands by the city desk, newspaper in hand, his shirt-sleeves gleaming snow-white in the oblique radiance. His bearing is respectful, but slightly indifferent.

"I'll see to everything," he says.

"Well, good-night."

"Good-night."

Barlow, passing through the room from his locker, makes the floor creak with his heavy and hurried stride. He looks strange with his coat on. His hat clings to his large head in a sort of trepidation. He is in great haste to catch his elevated train, which passes the building at 6:03 exactly; so that he flings to Josslyn a hurried farewell, and he attacks the swinging-door impatiently, as though it might frustrate him in getting away. Following more tranquilly at his heels is a reporter, Wallace, who fondles a cigarette and pauses a few paces from Josslyn.

"Commiserations, old chap. Any news?"

"No, replies Josslyn. "He might live the night out; can't tell."

"How late you stuck?"

"Eleven o'clock—if nothing happens."

Wallace shrugs, lights his cigarette, departs.

Josslyn is left alone, except for Dunstane, the Cub, who is sprawling at his desk, yawning, and reading a moving picture magazine.

It is the Late Watch. Josslyn is in charge of it, and the Cub is his staff. An august person, no other than the governor of this, our state, lies dying in the capital two hundred miles away. Death, when it releases him, will release Josslyn also.

[II]

THE Late Watch. There hover about this institution suggestions of gloom, of boredom, of mystery, of anticipation, of reflection. The Late Watch is uncanny. It hints of the unusual, possibly the dreadful. One knows that there has been a full day's work; a complete procession of the ordinary episodes and crises of a day. There has been a summing up and a final punctuation of all that twelve hours could do. And yet there persists an unfinished event, a shadow of probability, so potent that here are Josslyn and his "staff," still on duty. The allegro of the day's action is to have a coda—that is, if "he" dies. The city is now hurrying home, weary, full-stuffed with impressions and experiences. The street-cars and the elevated trains are carrying home the crowds, who throw off rapidly their interest in affairs. The city is bound for sleep. But the city will awaken again, will spring up alert, wondering, regretful, voluble, if "he" dies. At least, this is the theory of the Late Watch.

In the capital the august person lies on a carved bedstead in the middle of a huge, high-ceilinged chamber on the second floor of the "executive mansion." He lies as though dead, barely breathing. Each breath is an affair of state. It is noted by physicians and secretaries. The words "he still breathes" are passed out from the group of physicians, narrow-eyed by the bed, to the secretaries who murmur and wait in the ante-chamber. Reporters prowl around, murmuring with the secretaries; and there are messengers who sit against the wall, snoring into their caps; and in a farther room, there are telegraph operators who lounge in front of instruments, and listen to strange, irrelevant messages as they pass. Thus evening closes down over the capital, and over the executive mansion, and in that domain also there is a Late Watch.

The wires, hissing with divers things, and making long, mysterious streaks over meadows and along railroad tracks, connect the capital with Josslyn's newspaper office, as with some hundreds of others. Here in Josslyn's office there is a room where a telegraph operator waits, half listening to chatter from New York and Philadelphia, ready to spring when there emerges the call that is for his ear alone. From his chair the operator can see through the open door Josslyn's gray head and the contour of Josslyn's oval cheek, under the desk-light. It will be ten strides only to Josslyn's side. It will be a "quick flash."

Thus the two Late Watches are joined. There is a chain of efficiency and professional pride all the way from the sleepless physicians and the nimble secretaries to our office and to Josslyn.

"Will 'he' die? Will 'he' live out the night?" these questions are written huge both in the capital and here. But the answer is written elsewhere.

[III]

IN the face of this mystery, which is only artificially greater than the fate of some dipsomaniac now dying in the county hospital, a very notable calmness prevails in the news-room.

Josslyn sits reading. He has put on a pair of horn-rimmed spectacles, which he wears for night work only. He is held by his book; not a muscle of his serious, youthfully-cast, but greying face moves. Deliberately he turns pages; thoughtfully he absorbs the printed lines, missing none. After all, it must be that what he is reading surpasses in importance the question whether the governor will die. A circle of electric light and a solemn book form Josslyn's radius.

Dunstane, the Cub, is restless. He flicks the pages of his magazine, and throws it away. He discovers a deck of cards, and spreads them out for solitaire. Abandoning this, he yawns twice, with an impatient "yawp!" at the end, and gets up.

"Say Josslyn——"

"H—m?"

"How long do you think we'll be stuck?"

Before replying, Josslyn has to unfasten his mind from the page.

"H—m? Oh, we're due to stay until eleven—if nothing happens."

"Well, do you think the old beggar'll last till then?"

"How can I tell, kid?"

"Well, I thought there might be some late bulletin or something—my gosh, I didn't sign up for this sort of stuff. If this is newspaper work, gimme back my army job."

Josslyn is again deep in his book. The Cub thrusts his hands into his poskets, and makes a turn about the news-room, part of the way in dance-step. Returning, apparently much brightened, he says: "Say, Josslyn, did I tell you about that girl that I—oh, you're reading."

Josslyn turns a page. The Cub walks away to a window, over-looking the street. Down there the stragglers in the army of home-going workers are footing it to the street-cars, or waiting to cross between the close procession of teams and motor-cars. A cross-hatch of electric lights plays among the crowds. The shadows are black and eccentric. Above the roof-tops a huge sign flares out: "The Wonder Theater."

It is all very gay, the Cub thinks. The burble of the street comes to him softened, but winning.

He can hear the laughter of girls, the rough glad warnings of teamsters from their howdahs, the shriek of whistles at the crossing, the whole entrancing, fluid voice of the city. It is going somewhere. It is free.

But he, the Cub, is a prisoner.

He scowls at the clock on the wall; the beastly, crawling clock. He compares the clock fantastically with "Old Josslyn," the stationary and reconciled Josslyn, who can read, read, read while a golden evening spreads its pageantry in the streets. He is vexed with the idea that Josslyn can so calmly await the Event, and the release. Will he ever be like Josslyn? Good God, no! There's got to be something happening when he's around, you bet! If it doesn't happen he'll make it. This room, with its atmosphere of dead effort, is intolerable . . . . Nothing to do; nothing to do. Supposing even that the "flash" comes, he will accomplish nothing, unless to carry a message somewhere. Josslyn will do it all . . . And what if they wait until eleven o'clock, and no "flash" comes? Worse and worse. Then they will have waited for nothing at all . . . .

During these reflections the Cub stretches his powerful young arms, and rises on his toes, in gymnastics. Suddenly he comes down on his heels. The telegraph key is raining taps. The Cub becomes rigid. He thrusts his head toward the calm, moon-faced operator as the latter emerges

from his room. The Cub takes a step, and snatches the message from the telegraph man, and reads:
"Bulletin: 6:30 p. m.
Temperature, 101; pulse, 120; respiration, 32.
Morphy.
Jennings."

The Cub, scowling, conveys the yellow slip to Josslyn's desk and lays it in front of him.

"There you are; still alive."

Josslyn glances at the message; nods.

"All right. Thanks."

The room is again silent, save for the clock-tick.

[IV]

THERE now sounds in the hall a clatter of clumsy feet, and a swashing sound. In a few minutes a group of scrub-women, bearing pails, push into the news-room, and go to work, quite oblivious of Josslyn and the Cub. They are stout, shapeless creatures, with lank hair piled on their heads; and they murmur among themselves, in some foreign tongue, gossip of their own world.

The Cub, with hands in his trousers pockets, eyes the women with disgust. They slosh water toward where Josslyn sits; they move furniture about firmly and efficiently. At length they advance upon Josslyn, and he is forced to get up, with his finger in his book. Thus interrupted, he percieves the Cub and his fevers. His eyes soften.

It's pretty hard to do nothing, isn't it?" says

he to his "staff." "Go out and smoke if you want to. I can manage alone. Well, then," as the Cub shakes his head, "stick around, and think of your sins . . . . There's a lot of this sort of hum-drum in the newspaper business." They perch side by side upon an unmolested desk. "Wait until you've hung two days and nights for a verdict. Wait till you've done a stunt at a national convention. . . . . The Late Watch was invented to prove the whimsicality of events; in other words, the fact that no law, nor any human control, rules News. You take it as it comes. You wait."

(The Cub will say tomorrow: "You ought to've heard the string of philosophical bunk Josslyn handed me.")

"I've been reading history," goes on the elder man. "History tells you how there are long grey days and nights while an event piles up, and then comes the event, like a lightning stroke; and there is a roll of thunder; then the monotonous rumble of ordinary affairs goes on again. The big men of history were always there to deal the lightning-stroke—or to get struck. That's newspaper work; you're there, or else you aren't."

Josslyn smiles, and, folding his arms, gazes about the news-room—scene of all his achievements.

"I suppose so," returns the Cub aimlessly.

There is a diversion. The Drunkard enters, involving himself quaintly with the outgoing scrubwomen and their pails. Making a successful detour, he approaches Josslyn and the Cub. His expression is demure, but a satanic twinkle as of triumph—or maybe of strategy—dwells in his black eyes. He is not very drunk.

"Is th'—th' old beezer—dead yet?" he inquires, clutching the edge of a desk.

"No," returns Josslyn shortly.

"Can I—can I—do anything for you?"

"No," Josslyn does not turn his head.

The Drunkard looks reproachfully at Josslyn, perceives he is implacable, and sits down outside the circle of electric light. And he grins weakly at the Cub, as though he would address him. But he recalls in time that he owes him money.

Another diversion. A printer, wearing a leather apron and huge shoes slashed to ease his feet, shambles in from the corridor. He is well on in middle age, deliberate of movement, and wears the aspect of a professional buffoon. He waves a blackened hand at the Drunkard, glances about the desks for newspapers which he may purloin, and at last addresses Josslyn:

"So he ain't dead yet?"

"Not yet, Billy."

"Well . . . . I was wondering if I could go to dinner."

There is a brief dialogue about ways and means which postpones the printer's design of going to dinner. In the meantime another man has entered the room. He is a deep-chested bullock with a countenance both determined and good-humored. He walks in with a solid tread very much like the Old Man's; and in fact he belongs to the Old Man's generation of never-say-die.

"Well, ain't the governor goin' to kick in tonight, after all?" is his paraphrase of the stock query.

Josslyn merely smiles.

The stout man seats himself as though it were his first pause that day. And perhaps it is, for he works in the depths of the building, watching the streams of papers as they come from the presses and directing the flow into wagons and trucks. He is "the mailing-room boss," who, it is said, never sits down.

"What say we start a little game?" he grins.

The Cub and the Drunkard look alive, but Josslyn shakes his head, with, "You know the Old Man barred it the last time."

The mailing-room boss shrugs his fleshy shoulders, but drops the subject.

"Well, it's many a late watch you and I've had together," he remarks to Josslyn. "Do you remember the time we hung out for the Pope's death ten years ago? And things got balled up, too. You flashed me over the 'phone 'Pope dead,' sure as you're born; and we started th' paper out with a whoop. Two seconds, and there were you on the 'phone again. 'Kill 'em,' says you. I remember how your voice sounded."

"And I remember how you swore," counters Josslyn.

"We got back all but about three hundred papers, though," says the mailing-room man, smacking his lips at the memory of that battle. "The Old Man never heard about it till weeks afterward."

The Cub's eyes grow bright and wondering at these memoirs. The Drunkard now snores.

"Speakin' of long chances and all that," pipes up the printer, "I was a boy in the old Times office when Grant died. I remember the night darn well, bet you. We was on all night, an' the gang played seven-up. Well, sir, I'll never forget it. It got toward morning, and I remember old Poison Green, foreman in them days, was a dollar an' a quarter to the bad. Hadn't been for that I reckon we'd 'a broke up the watch. But we had a wire strung to—to—where was it Grant died?"

"Mount McGregor," someone prompts.

"Yes, an' we had a full first page made up an' stereotyped. Well, it got on toward mornin', and there was Green an' Foxy Dunlap, the editor, and a telegraph operator there. The wire was sputterin' away in the other room. Suddenly, just as Green starts to rake in a pot that would 'a put him even, the operator pricks up his head, like a horse, and he jumps up and hollers: 'Grant's dead!' 'n Poison Green gives a whoop and heads for th' composin' room, and Dunlap goes an' whistles down th' tube to th' mailin' room, and only after they'd let the paper go did they think to ask what the operator knew about it all, and then they find he'd only heard a flash goin' over the wire, an' it might be true, an' it mightn't. But it turned out all right——"

"Come, Billy," says Josslyn. "You don't mean to say they let the extra go on a message for some other paper?"

"It might 'a been for some other paper. It might 'a been for th' governor o' Timbuctoo. Anyways, they let 'er go, and they scooped the town. But old Poison Green never did collect all of that pot."

There is mild laughter over this; then yawns, and a stretching of arms. Josslyn alone is thoughtful, wide-awake. He says to the mailing-room boss, "You got that dummy plate all safe downstairs?"

"Nobody can release it but me," returns the boss, surveying his big fist. "If they did, they'd get killed—or worse."

(Even the Cub understands that a dummy plate is a prepared page, stereotyped, ready for the press.)

More yawns.

"He'll hang on till morning," predicts the mailing-room man, wagging his head. "Them politicians are tough."

He and the printer stroll out of the room, muttering. The Cub obtains permission to eat dinner. The Drunkard follows him into the hall, waveringly. Josslyn is left alone.

[V]

ALONE, he is suddenly the prey of nervous forebodings. That was only his shell that the Cub saw him in. Within the shell he is a ganglion of emotions, foresights and fears. Though he "hung out" for a thousand verdicts and kept late watches on a thousand death-beds, he would ever be the same. The mere presence of the incalculable works upon his brain; the consciousness of an approaching "flash" sets up a painful tingle of dread.

He paces the room slowly, angry with himself. Surely, he has faced this sort of responsibility often enough. By now he should be able to apply the fatalism of the profession; he should be hardened, and should say "I don't care a damn." Indeed, he pretends that he doesn't care. He says to himself: "What if something did go wrong? Suppose I did let go the extra before the governor died? I shouldn't die of it myself, should I?" But this thought only makes him aware that he would care, terribly. He would—he would resign next morning, of course; he would leave town, that he would. He would bury himself and his humiliation in oblivion.

Well, what can go wrong? How can anything possibly go wrong? "Let's see," he reasons, pacing the floor: "The operator will get the flash; he'll write it out, must have him write it out; then a telephone call to the mailing-room, and"—that ends Josslyn's responsibility. Simple. Inevitable.

But—the correspondent at the capital might blunder. Josslyn might get his tongue twisted at the telephone. Something . . . . the queerest things have been known to occur in these Late Watches. Everybody keyed to a high pitch. Everybody inclined to gamble . . . .

He pulls himself together. But he cannot return to his book; nor can he maintain any definite flow of thought. The mystery is greater than that merely of "When will he die?" The sense of helplessness before this or any other unfinished event is overpowering. The whole thing is part of the great veil which Life draws over profound matters, and with which it mocks men and at the same time perpetuates them. Josslyn is helpless before it. His grasp on simple, ordinary ideas is disorganized. As he stands at the window, spectator of the night where dwell thousands of creatures, as helpless as he, his fingers are a little clenched, his face frowns, "When—when will it come?"

But this is newspaper work. Would he exchange it for the dull certainty of a book-keeper's desk? No, though it may wreck him some day, though

it almost certainly leads to failure and can
scarcely lead, even for a day, to glory, this is better
than the work which one can control by certain
processes, and fold away in a pigeon-hole. No!
Face out the eccentric future, breast the chances
of success or disgrace: This is worth many a
"tamer" job.

Thus in the complex soul of Josslyn there rises
the courage of a gamester with life, challenging
and making way against the weakness of sick
imagination.

Suddenly he whirls. The operator has spoken.

Or did he speak? The long half-dark newsroom is full of phantoms, of eerie voices.

"It's all right," calls the operator from his
room. "I thought I got the flash. It was a
mistake."

Josslyn turns again to the window. The sky,
sallow with electric flares, is ghostly. The rooftops, outlined against it, are broken into turmoil,
like waves. A turmoil of things guessed.

[VI]

THERE is a step in the room and Josslyn, turning, beholds the Star, who walks rapidly to
the mail-box, finds a letter, and leaves the room
as quickly as he entered it. Josslyn would have
liked him to stay, for the Star is cheerful company, and he knows nothing of responsibility and
its tremors. But the Star is only passing through,

and the scent of his cigarette, smoked in despite of rules, is all that remains of him.

Josslyn falls to thinking of his comrades; not only of the Star, but of the incorrigible Drunkard, and the comic Cub; of the globe-trotting Goode, now somewhere on a rolling sea; of Barlow, sweet-tempered and gruff-spoken; of Brown, the young city editor, and Emmett, the pervasive news editor; of Campbell, the philosopher, and of the grey Poet; of the Old Man, who has never quite forgiven Josslyn, yet cherishes him; and of all the others, notable or not, the quick-silver company of the news-room, bound together in a great pride of work, but expressing it in growls and barks of apparent displeasure.

Others besides the men of the news-room come to Josslyn's mind. He thinks of the intent compositors at their linotypes, the grave, leisurely printers in the "ad-room." He remembers with sympathy and fondness certain stereotypers, elderly men perhaps, clad in smeared overalls, grey-faced with early rising. His fancy descends to the depths, among the proud, vociferous presses, and embraces the big-handed fellows who jovially control the cylinders. And he thinks with a blend of pity and humor of the aged "information man" in the hall, snow-bearded, punctilious, and humble. He remembers many a sharp-eyed, swaggering driver of wagons or trucks, men who drive in all weathers, and always arrive.

And he thinks even of spinsterly book-keepers in the business office, doing a man's work. And he regards with particular affection the taciturn old fellow who runs the elevator, up and down, up and down . . . . There is no end to their number, bowed or bustling at the common task, all through the rooms, corridors, basements of the Press building; these people who move incessantly, like Josslyn himself, slaves of the clock.

His regard for these people is very great. Yes, he is among friends, day and night. What more can a man ask? He thinks, "Perhaps there is some of all these people in me. I must have absorbed a bit from all, during these years."

And above this, there is the inexplicable bond that holds him to the paper itself; there is his curious affection for an inanimate mass of pulp—the paper. He will fight for it, not for himself. He will not let it stumble. It——

What's that?

Yes: "Governor dead!"

The operator bounds from his chair. He has scrawled the two words. Josslyn, on a quick stride, snatches the paper. He travels the room in leaps, and deftly lifts the telephone receiver. There is a tremendous second of waiting, then:

"George! Let 'er go! Governor dead!"

In the moments while he dashed down the room, in that instant at the telephone, he has thought of nothing, he has had not a single tremor; action has sublimated the doubting Josslyn.

He stands beside the desk, mentally numb. The flash has come, the dreaded moment has passed, as softly and nonchalantly as a drop of rain. The silent room belies the fact that the clouds have emitted a bolt. The clock-hands seem to stand still.

But presently there is a thunder from below, a churning of mighty monsters. And there come up, distantly, from the streets the wails of newsboys, crying the tidings that the august person breathes no more.

And the Cub, entering a moment later, finds Josslyn smiling.

[VII]

So it goes, the dim procession of days and nights, illumined by great flares from the world beyond. The presses roar endlessly, in time with the eternity of news.

THE END